The Rainbow Picnic

by the same author

Biography
THE DUCHESS OF JERMYN STREET (Rosa Lewis)
EMERALD AND NANCY : Lady Cunard and her Daughter

Autobiography
MERCURY PRESIDES
THE NEAREST WAY HOME

Fiction
THE ADONIS GARDEN

Iris at Lake Kammer (*photograph by Cecil Beaton*)

DAPHNE FIELDING

The Rainbow Picnic

A PORTRAIT OF
Iris Tree

EYRE METHUEN · LONDON

*First published 1974
by Eyre Methuen Ltd
11 New Fetter Lane, EC4P 4EE
© 1974 Daphne Fielding
Printed in Great Britain by
Clarke, Doble & Brendon Ltd
Plymouth*

ISBN 0 413 28520 0

For DIANA COOPER with love

Contents

Author's Acknowledgements 11
Foreword 13

PART ONE

1 The Parents 19
2 The Buttercup Fields of Childhood 30
3 Student at the Slade 44
4 America 60
5 Curtis Moffat 69
6 England Again 75
7 The Miracle 86
8 Friedrich Ledebur 92

PART TWO

9 Austria and Ireland 99
10 The Chekhov Theatre Studio 111
11 The Glass Bubble 120
12 Personal View of Iris 128
13 Quest for the Eventual Tower 135
14 Last Picnic Grounds 142
15 Where the Rainbow Ends 152

Index 157

Illustrations

Endpapers 'Rainbow Picnic' by Iris Tree. Among the picnickers are Iris, Friedrich and Virginia
Frontispiece Iris at Lake Kammer by Cecil Beaton

facing page
1a and b   Iris's parents, Sir Herbert and Lady Tree   32
2a   Iris as a child   33
2b   Iris as an art student by Curtis Moffat   33
2c   Viola Tree   33
3a   Epstein bust of Iris   48
3b   Portrait of Iris by Dora Carrington   48
4   Sybil Hart-Davis   49
5   Curtis Moffat   64
6a   Viola and Iris in fancy dress by Curtis Moffat   65
6b   Iris and Diana Manners   65
7a   Friedrich and Iris   80
7b   Friedrich and Boon   80
8   Iris in California   81

between pages 144 and 145
9a   Ivan Moffat
9b   Iris and Oonagh Oranmore
9c   Iris, Boon and Captain Eric Meiville

10a Iris in Rome
10b Iris reading 'Tiger, tiger, burning bright'
11 Iris and Aguri, her Belgian sheepdog
12 Last photograph of Iris by Cecil Beaton

Acknowledgement and thanks for permission to reproduce the photographs are due to the marchioness of Bath for the endpapers; to Sir Cecil Beaton for the frontispiece and plate 12; to the Radio Times Hulton Picture Library for plates 1a and 1b; to Mrs Kate Townend for plate 3b; to Madame Yvonde for plate 4; to Oonagh Lady Oranmore and Browne for plates 9b and 9c; and to Derek Hill for plates 10a and 10b. Plate 3a is from *Jacob Epstein* by Richard Buckle; plate 6a is from *Castles in the Air* by Viola Tree; and plate 6b is from *The Light of Common Day* by Diana Cooper.

Author's Acknowledgements

First of all I wish to express my gratitude to Lady Diana Cooper for her help and encouragement; also to the marchioness of Bath for her prompt response to all my questions, the loan of letters written to her mother, Viola Tree, and the sketch by Iris from which the end papers were made.

Ivan Moffat gave me access to his mother's few remaining papers, provided photographs taken by his father, and wrote the evocative word picture of Iris at the beginning of this book.

Iris's second son, Dr Christian Ledebur, helped me to follow his mother back into the past; while Lady Cory-Wright shed light on the Tree sisters' childhood.

I am particularly indebted to Count Ledebur for showing me letters, lending me photographs and reminiscing to the benefit of this book.

Mrs Daphne Field gave me a detailed description of life at the Chekhov Theatre Studio, both in Devonshire and California.

Sir Rupert Hart-Davis generously allowed me to draw on a collection of letters written to his mother, Sybil Hart-Davis, and very kindly read the proofs of this book, and Mrs Gilbert Russell lent me letters that Iris wrote to her throughout their life-long friendship.

I am also indebted to Mrs Eileen B. Sayers who wrote to me describing her life with Iris while she was nurse to her second son, Boon.

Professor Quentin Bell gave me permission to publish a letter written by Clive Bell and told me there were other letters from Iris to his father preserved among the Charleston Papers at King's College, Cambridge, which the librarian, Dr A. N. L. Munby, produced for me, thereby opening up a fresh path through the wood.

Hesketh Pearson's biography of Sir Herbert Beerbohm was an invaluable guide to the early relationship between Iris's parents.

Mr Derek Hill and Oonagh Lady Oranmore and Browne generously took the risk of allowing me to steam photographs out of their treasured albums, and Mr Richard Morphet kindly allowed me to quote from his personal diary.

I also thank Sir John Betjeman and Lord David Cecil for their expert appreciation of *The Marsh Picnic*.

My husband, Xan Fielding, gave me constructive criticism on reading my manuscript, and Miss Solita Solano also made helpful suggestions.

Miss Miriam Rosenthal gave pertinent advice regarding some cuts and clarification.

Miss Heather Willings typed the manuscript and eliminated a few howlers. For all this help I count myself most fortunate.

Foreword

Iris Tree was the most truly Bohemian person I have ever known: totally unconcerned about public opinion, material matters and conventional society. Romance was the star she followed until the end of her days.

The heritage of her blood was strong, as was her sister Viola's early influence upon her character: her father and mother were both wits who delighted in playing with words and turning a phrase. From the Beerbohms she inherited an untarnishable youthfulness of spirit, while her mother imbued her with a certain sensibility which made her shrink from brashness and coarseness in speech or behaviour. I have therefore described with some detail the lives of her parents and elder sister.

Although she was known to many as a poet and could be called a celebrity, she nevertheless remained a private individual. Unusually gifted, she perhaps spread her talents over too broad a surface in her search for the form of expression she needed. Her letters were so evocative that she seemed to spring out of the envelope as one opened it. They have been preserved by those who were fortunate enough to receive them, and happily I have been given access to many.

I did not meet Iris until the early 1930s, and so can give a first-hand account of her only in the second part of this book.

In all humility, with sincere admiration and affection, I have attempted to perpetuate her in this portrait; for we shall not see her like again.

DAPHNE FIELDING

La Galerie des Pâtres, Uzès
December 1973

'There are few things as sad,' she said, 'as the clothes of a dead dandy. Or harder to describe.'

Half beauty, half broken doll, knight-errant gypsy, hair-helmet turning slowly through red, gold to faded yellow, while her eyes – once lighthouses – became the sockets of dreams; striped skirts, champagne shirts, gold and silver sequins, parti-coloured stockings, and in 1925 the first of faded jeans, then a plum-coloured cloak, then a black, then a night-dress transparent over dying limbs. Her gift was words.

'Iris,' I said at last, at half-past six, 'would you now like anything to drink?'

'I would, maybe – yes – I think I would like – '

'Yes, yes – what?'

'All right, then – a little vodka, perhaps, to keep me quiet.'

Ivan, elder son.

Part One

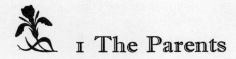 # 1 The Parents

Thurnham Court, an Elizabethan house standing at the foot of the Kentish downs, had once been taken by Lord Byron so that he could be near his mistress, Lady Oxford. The windows looked out over distant fields of corn. Maidstone was a four-mile carriage drive away. There were wooded walks and bridle-paths for rides across gently undulating downland.

In the summer of 1882, Thurnham Court had another tenant – Mr Julius Beerbohm, a distinguished London corn merchant – and in this romantic setting the last stages of an ardent and stormy courtship terminated in a pretty country wedding. The bride was nineteen-year-old Maud Holt, an orphan who had been brought up by her elder sister; the bridegroom was Herbert Beerbohm, Julius's twenty-six-year-old son.

They had met first at a fancy-dress ball and were at once attracted to each other. Throughout that summer the wistful cadences of his voice lingered in her imagination and she invented excuses for walking past the Garrick Club, in the hope of seeing him at the window. Finally she wrote to him, asking if he thought her success on the amateur stage warranted her trying to become a professional actress. His reply was not encouraging:

The Rainbow Picnic

My dear Miss Holt,
   Don't go on the stage unless you feel you *must*. We shall meet again in the autumn.

Yours sincerely,
H.B.T.

But it was not until a winter afternoon that he came to tea in her Orchard Street rooms, where she was chaperoned by her landlady. On his next visit there was no chaperone and they read poetry to each other in front of the fire. A few weeks later he proposed and was accepted.

Their first tiffs were over poets. Maud was a devotee of Browning, whom Herbert found 'mystically meaningless . . . my mind seems Browning-barren'. But he agreed with her over Tennyson and sent her a copy of *Maud* in which he marked his favourite passages.

His parents were straight away enchanted by the grace of her wand-like figure with its trim waist, her deep-set dark-blue eyes, fresh complexion and small head crowned with softly curling brown hair. They noted and appreciated the determination shown in her strong chin. They were charmed by her delightful singing voice. They were impressed that she was also teaching classics at Queen's College, Harley Street. She had been preparing for an academic career with Girton as her goal, but now, wishing to share Herbert's life, she was more than ever determined to go on the stage.

The young couple often entertained the Beerbohms after dinner with recitations, dialogues and imitations, Maud's spontaneous talent appearing at its best when she and Herbert improvised together. After giving up his job in the family business and having reached the professional stage by way of amateur theatricals, he was just beginning to be known as an actor. At first his father had disapproved. 'An actor can be tolerated only if he is at the top of the tree,' he told his son. It was this remark that inspired Herbert to assume the name of Tree. With his red hair and light-blue eyes fringed with sandy eyelashes, he was not the conventional matinée idol; but his stature was impressive, his teeth perfect, his voice attractive, his conversation entertain-

The Parents

ing, so that whenever he talked – and he talked a great deal – his features became animated and he appeared handsome.

His father, a naturalized Englishman of German, Dutch and Lithuanian descent, had spent his early life in Germany and, on coming to England, had set himself up as a grain merchant in the City. He made the most of a long bachelordom and often went to Paris, where his fine looks earned him the nickname of '*Monsieur Superbe-homme*'. At the age of forty-five he married Constantia Draper, a young woman with ethereal looks and charm but who was so vague that she was likely to drift around with her shoe-laces untied; when someone remarked on this, she merely murmured, 'I like them untied'. After her early death Julius promptly married her sister Eliza, who had lived with the family for some years, helping Constantia to run the house and bring up the four children. The children found a second mother in their aunt, and in due course Eliza had two girls, Agnes and Dora, and Max, the youngest of all.

The Beerbohms were unusually clannish and preferred their own company to that of friends and acquaintances. They would listen to one another with rapt attention, their interest and amusement being none the less genuine for showing the conventional courtesy more usually reserved for strangers. They invented their own personal mythology as well as a private anthology of games and jokes. The atmosphere was described as 'a mixture of Lear and Thackeray'.* The girls had a 'greenery-yallery' pre-Raphaelite aura. Agnes yearned for a harp; Dora modelled herself on Kate Greenaway illustrations, wearing long sage-green and copper-coloured skirts; while their mother dressed like the widowed Queen Victoria. Such was the family circle which opened to enfold Maud Holt.

Not surprisingly, Maud's and Herbert's temperaments frequently clashed. Her exuberance would often turn to melancholy, while he was an unfailing optimist. After their quarrels she would brood in silence, magnifying the cause, while he raged briefly, forgave and forgot. These squalls were usually caused by her busybody friends and relations, 'a little more than kin and less than kind', repeating some scandal about her betrothed, who,

* David Cecil, *Max* (Constable, 1964).

newly in the public eye, had become a target for gossip. Her peace of mind was easily disturbed and she needed constant reassurance of his love.

Shortly before the wedding he wrote to her:

> I was very sorry, darling, to leave you this evening – on Sunday I hope we shall have a long day together. I will endeavour to turn the bright side towards you – it is not always day! but it is not that the sun does not shine – rather it is the earth that revolves and makes it night.

In July 1882, Maud took her sister to Aix to convalesce after a serious illness. Herbert had arranged to join them later. Meanwhile more scandal reached her and she stopped writing, leaving him puzzled and disturbed by her silence, until he learned from his stepmother that Maud was again doubting him. This time he took a firmer line:

> ... I gave you to understand, when I first asked you to care for me, – that my past life had not been entirely unworldly. I repented what I had done and you forgave me. – I have endeavoured to make every reparation for the error committed before I knew you, and I have been true and loyal to you. There was never at any time the slightest claim upon me and I have recently taken the steps to remove even the possibility of a shadow in the future. Can I do more? Have I hitherto been impatient of your reproaches and the attacks of your friends? To whom do you owe your allegiance – to them or to me? It is for you now to say – I do not care to enter into competition with them – nor will I allow you to despise me, did I not demand your entire trust and a love which is not regulated by acquaintances – as this may be demanding too much, I am anxious to release you from such a bondage – for I assure you that if I honour and value your love, I also honour and value my own dignity.
>
> Your affectionate Herbert

But before he had posted the letter he received a telegram from Maud:

> Come if you like directly.

So he then sent the letter, enclosing a postscript:

> My dearest – since writing I have received your telegram. – I shall come to you at once. Nevertheless I think it right to send this letter – I hope you won't think it harsh – and certainly I think it best not to keep it back – I shall be with you then, very soon – my dearest. I shall telegraph you again tomorrow when I leave London – meantime God bless you.

Nevertheless, after he had announced his arrival at Aix by an affectionate note in which he begged her to see him soon, she let a whole day elapse before sending for him. Their quarrel made up, they spent an idyllic fortnight together and decided to get married as soon as possible.

Shortly afterwards he wrote to her:

> I am glad to tell you that I played better tonight, perhaps better than I have played in my life, and there were shouts of 'Bravo, Tree!' at the fall of the curtain and of which I felt very proud. I only hope the other gods will shout 'Bravo, Tree!' when the curtain falls on our little domestic drama.

Maud spent the night before the wedding at Thurnham Court. Herbert was acting and arrived only just in time for the ceremony, his little half-brother Max acting as best man because his full brother Julius was delayed abroad.

The wedding bells pealed as the bride and bridegroom came out of church and walked the short distance to the rambling house, down a petal-strewn path and under rustic arches erected in their honour, made of autumn foliage pranked with the mauve stars of Michaelmas daisies and rosetted with chrysanthemums and dahlias.

At the wedding breakfast they sat in throne-like chairs decorated with nosegays and garlands of flowers woven by Agnes and Dora. The feast included syllabub, which Max found all the more exotic when Herbert remarked, 'They sound so biblical – Syllabub the son of Syllabub reigneth in his stead'.

Since Herbert was acting there was no question of a honeymoon. He and Maud went straight back to his lodgings in Burlington Gardens, for which he paid three guineas a week. Their married life passed through a variety of climates but, like an oak that resists the tempests, the wood weathered and the roots held fast.

It was as natural as breathing for Herbert to court a woman who attracted him and, with charm allied to stage presence, he was usually irresistible. Maud realized this, but the streak of puritanism in her nature made her unable to accept his gallantries to others; and whenever she sensed a rival she became clumsy and tactless. Furthermore she made the mistake of cleaving to him in his professional as well as social life. He continued to disapprove of her making a stage career, and gave her no assistance or encouragement. Through her own manœuvres, however, she obtained the part of Hester Gould in *The Millionaire*, in which she proved to have a gift for high comedy. She received flattering notices and Herbert, after reading them, said (only half in jest): 'I hope this doesn't mean you're going to be more famous than me.... I couldn't have that, you know.'

Their combined salaries enabled them to take a house. Their first real home was at 4 Wilton Place, leading out of Grosvenor Place. Both of them were born hosts and enjoyed entertaining a growing circle of diverse friends; their small supper parties after the theatre soon became the fashion with Victorian society. But when Herbert found himself out of work they had to sub-let the house and move into a borrowed flat. Herbert's sister, Constance, lent them money and they paid her back in Sheraton chairs. During these lean days Maud kept careful accounts, noting the purchase of 'snowdrops and clean collars for Herbert', and doled out small sums of pocket money to him – sometimes only half-a-crown a week. But with Herbert in a new part they were soon back in Belgravia; such contrasts became a recurring pattern.

In March 1884 he had his first big success, playing the Reverend Robert Spalding in *The Private Secretary*, a farce adapted from the German by Charles Hawtrey. At first he was not at ease in the part, but improved on it by burlesquing, gagging and improvising. At one rehearsal, while standing in the wings with Maud beside him, he had yet another bright idea for underlining the character of the Reverend Spalding.

The Parents

'Quick, get me a blue ribbon!'* he said.

Maud looked around and, seeing nothing suitable, ripped a piece of cloth from the sleeve of her white gown, made a dash upstairs to the paint-room and dipped it in a pot of blue wash, getting back just in time to hand Herbert the emblem.

The play had a rewardingly long run, enabling the Trees to take a house in Cheyne Walk, where, in July 1884, their first child, Viola, was born.

Soon after her birth they made friends with W. S. Gilbert and his wife, and the two couples spent many weekends together. Gilbert made a great fuss of Viola when she was a small child but she did not always appreciate his attentions. One day she refused to kiss him.

'Oh do kiss Gilly, darling,' her father pleaded. 'Daddy loves Gilly.'

'Then Daddy kiss Gilly,' she retorted.

Gilbert was a difficult and touchy man, but Maud, tactful with everyone except her husband, understood him and they kept up a skittish correspondence, in which he addressed her as 'D.K.L.' (Dear Kind Lady), signing his letters, 'Your amusing friend D.K.G.' (Dear Kind Gentleman). Sometimes he added: 'Who loves you as he didn't ought to'. The flirtatious note in their friendship irritated Herbert.

In 1886 Herbert joined F. R. Benson's company for a summer season at Bournemouth, to play the parts of Iago and Sir Peter Teazle. Maud was engaged to play Portia and Lady Teazle. She and Mrs Benson spent most mornings on the beach, where Viola would pick up pebbles which she presented one after the other to her mother, who thanked her as earnestly as though these were gifts of exceptional value: 'Clever, clever girl!' Then, turning to Mrs Benson, she added, "You always tell children and men they are clever; I don't know why, but I know it's expected.'

Maud was never satisfied for long with the atmosphere she created in their series of homes; no sooner was she settled than her actress's eye lighted on another suitably dramatic setting for Herbert.

* The badge of a teetotaller.

The Rainbow Picnic

In 1887 Herbert had a good year and took on the lease of the Haymarket Theatre, thereby gratifying his wish to become an actor-manager. He opened with a success, *The Red Lamp*, in which he played Demetrius, the head of the secret police. This role necessitated the most elaborate make-up, in which he had achieved an unusual degree of expertise. He always made up himself, and could achieve extraordinary transformations in a few minutes. As Viola said: 'It takes Daddy less time to make himself ugly than it takes Mother to make herself beautiful.'

There were times when Maud felt that the aura of fame surrounding him was a gulf between them and she became anxious and unsettled unless she too had a good part in his productions. He refused, however, to be cajoled into casting her in roles which did not really suit her; and this led to further quarrels and tears. Also there were scenes whenever she acted under his direction. She was wounded when he criticized her harshly in public, and resented his taking more trouble at rehearsals over other actresses than over her. When she was in the same cast as Julia Neilson, for instance, she complained to W. S. Gilbert that Herbert seemed more interested in the performance of this statuesque and popular actress than in her own. The 'dear kind gentleman' must have consoled her when he referred to the lovely Julia as 'Jowlier Neilson'.

Gilbert invariably sympathized with her and often disapproved of her husband. It must have been in such a mood that he visited Herbert in his dressing-room after the first night of the revival of Gilbert's comedy *Engaged*. Herbert was perspiring heavily, sweat running down his face, and Gilbert, instead of congratulating him on an excellent performance, merely said: 'At least your *skin* has been acting.' On another occasion, after Herbert had been playing Hamlet, Gilbert said: 'My dear fellow, I never saw anything so funny in my life, but you were not *vulgar*' (this remark gave rise to the subsequently popular expression, 'funny without being vulgar'). In this particular production Herbert had cast Maud as Ophelia; it was her happiest stage experience and her performance was enhanced by her touching voice singing Ophelia's plaintive songs.

The Parents

'Falling in love is largely a question of habit,' Herbert used to say, but although he made light of his gallantries Maud could not bring herself to ignore them. As his fame increased, the public eye fixed itself with an ever-increasing curiosity on his private life. She received cruel anonymous letters informing her of his love affairs. He was distressed that she should suffer so much through him and, after she had received a spate of particularly vicious letters, asked her in future to send all such letters to their friend and lawyer, Sir George Lewis.

In 1895 the Trees went to America on tour. The company travelled ahead of them, so Maud had Herbert to herself during the crossing. He was in his most charming and affectionate mood and she was idyllically happy. Nevertheless, at the end of the voyage he discovered her alone in their state-room weeping among the cabin trunks. He comforted her and, holding her in his arms, promised that such happiness would come to her again.

In America the Press reporters swarmed round them wherever they went, and Herbert was indulgent towards them, even enjoyed giving interviews. 'An American's house is an interviewer's castle,' he said.

Soon they were caught up on a merry-go-round of entertaining and constantly fêted by local Society. Maud was overwhelmed by the vitality and attentions of the many fashionable ladies and wrote to Viola:

> In my best brocade I feel quite shabby though I put on all Lady Granby's* jewels! *All* the grand ladies here are so joyous and full of fun as Margot Tennant — they dance about (most beautifully) and mimic people and shout and sing like children — so do the *very* smart, *very* stiff-collared, *very* correct young men — I suppose their climate makes them so light-hearted.

But the weather did little to raise her own spirits and she longed for a pause in the speeches and the banquets, the lectures and the travelling — just a little time in which she could be alone with Herbert.

* Later the duchess of Rutland.

The Rainbow Picnic

In Harvard he delighted the students at a lecture by delivering Hamlet's speech 'To be or not to be' in the style of Falstaff, followed by Falstaff's speech on honour given in the manner of Hamlet, for, he claimed, they both held the same philosophy. On another occasion he had a less appreciative audience who constantly interrupted him. Stepping to the front of the platform, he held up his hand and said:

'Excuse me, gentlemen, I have only a few more pearls to cast.'

His triumph was crowned in Washington, where he and Maud were received at the White House by President Cleveland.

Back in England, Maud established herself as a fashionable hostess at 77 Sloane Street. It was a very pretty house and she spent a large sum decorating it and putting in electric light. There were two drawing-rooms, one green and the other blue, and a dining-room panelled in bleached wood where half a dozen places were always set for a six o'clock supper before the theatre. On every other Sunday the leading lady and the author of whatever play was running at the Haymarket were invited to lunch. The Trees gave six big dinner parties a year at which the guests were invited to meet various celebrities such as the future Prime Minister and his wife – Mr and Mrs Asquith – Lily Elsie, or some literary figure like Anatole France.

Maud's style of entertaining was inventive and today she would probably have been called 'a trend setter'. She took endless trouble over her table arrangements: small bowls of anemones were placed in a long line down the middle; a Georgian doll's tea-service plate, filled with salted almonds, was set before each guest, also an individual pat of butter, salt cellar and pepper pot. She thought that food looked more appetizing on white plates, and her dinner-service was white Wedgwood with a raised pattern of leaves.

The American tour was repeated the following year, but this time Maud could not take part since she was pregnant. Holding Viola by the hand, she saw Herbert off at Southampton; as the ship moved away she threw a bunch of violets in its wake, in memory of the play *A Bunch of Violets* in which she had enchanted her American audiences the year before. She arranged that whenever this play was performed, a bunch of violets would be sent to Herbert's dressing-room with her love.

By this time the Trees had two daughters, Felicity having been born in 1895. Now they longed for a son. But their third child was a girl. Herbert was not back in London on 27 January 1897, when Iris was born, but as Maud wrote:

> The frost of our disappointment was soon melted away by the calm and inextinguishable sunshine of the newcomer.*

* Max Beerbohm, *Herbert Beerbohm Tree, Some Memories of Him and His Art* (Hutchinson, 1921).

2 The Buttercup Fields of Childhood

Opposite the Haymarket Theatre, on the site once occupied by a playhouse designed by Sir John Vanbrugh, stood a derelict opera house. Tree knew it was going to be demolished and visualized a theatre of his own arising in its place. In 1896, with the profits from his production of *Trilby*, in which he played Svengali, he bought the site.

Although he was such a bad businessman that he had to employ a manager to look after his monetary affairs, he had a genius for raising the wind, and so had Maud. During his absence in America she had successfully canvassed Sir Ernest Cassel and Mrs Bischofsheim,* and, on his return, Lord Rothschild, Carl Meyer and other rich friends were persuaded to invest in the enterprise. Tree himself subscribed £10,000 and, as proprietor, provided a further £5,000 a year for the ground-rent.

A handsome building of Portland stone, relieved with red granite and surmounted by a large copper dome, was eventually erected at a cost of £55,000 and named, in honour of the Queen, Her Majesty's Theatre. Tree was so proud of his achievement that he would stand for hours on the opposite side of the street, lost in blissful contemplation. If a friend passed by he would button-hole him and solicit his admiration. If no friend appeared,

* Friends of the Prince of Wales.

he would even accost strangers. One day a suffragette, misinterpreting his approach, knocked off his top hat and accused him of being no gentleman. 'Madam,' he replied, 'how can you know if I am no gentleman when you deprive me of the wherewithal of behaving like one?'

The interior decorations were by Romaine Walker, the colours dark red, cream and gold. The style was a pastiche of Louis XIV and Louis XV, and the finished effect was of elegance and comfort combined with efficiency. 'You feel that you are in a place where high scenes are to be enacted and dignified things are to be done,' wrote Bernard Shaw.

The audience were treated as if they were guests; no charge was made in the cloakrooms; the programmes were minor works of art. On first nights Tree himself wrote an introduction to the play, and commemorative engravings and photographs of the actors were given away. The male attendants were dressed in liveries similar to those worn by the footmen at Buckingham Palace, but the Prince of Wales objected and they were promptly changed. The orchestra was hidden by layered fronds of trees, and the lights dimmed almost imperceptibly. Furthermore the prices were lower than in other theatres.

Ignoring the theatrical superstition that Shakespeare, *Macbeth* in particular, brought bad luck, Tree set about presenting the most lavish and spectacular Shakespearean productions known on any stage. The first was *Julius Caesar*, which had not been seen in the West End for fifty years, furnished with costumes and décor by Lawrence Alma-Tadema. The play ran for five months – a long time in those days – and made a profit of £11,000. The average run of all Tree's productions was three months and he liked to take a play off when it was still drawing full houses.

Her Majesty's also provided him with a sanctuary in the great copper dome ('Herbert Tree at dome' was the wording Maud suggested for his invitation cards). The inner sanctum, where he often slept, was decorated with a frieze illustrating scenes from *Twelfth Night*. Walls lined with books provided him with a reference library. The large dining-room had a high raftered ceiling.

The Rainbow Picnic

He and Maud gave supper parties here after first nights, inviting patrons and the rank, style and brains of Society and 'High Bohemia'. He also cultivated the company of writers, for he was always on the lookout for authors to write plays for him. He had already commissioned *Beau Austin* from W. E. Henley and Robert Louis Stevenson, and their play *Macaire* was later performed at Her Majesty's.

Oscar Wilde was a frequent guest. Tree had staged *A Woman of No Importance* at the Haymarket, and played Lord Illingworth, whom Wilde had modelled on himself. In due course Tree used to invent epigrams in the manner of Wilde, who remarked, 'Every day dear Herbert becomes *de plus en plus Oscarisé* – a wonderful case of nature imitating art'.

Until a cook-housekeeper was installed, the food for these parties was sent in from the Carlton next door, which incidentally also provided scenic effects such as piping steam on to the stage. Thus the witches in *Macbeth* flew through swirling clouds of mist, and once one of them nearly died of pneumonia.*

Backstage at Her Majesty's phantasmagoric marvels were revealed to the Tree daughters and their friend Diana Manners:

> We were taken ... to performances and rehearsals as often as we liked, and were allowed to pester the actor-manager Tree (Mr Daddy to us) in his dressing-room. I do not think that he minded, although he had great occasion when we motley children plastered our baby chins with Henry VIII's hair, splashed our arms with great Caesar's blood and hee-hawed through Bottom's head.†

Far from minding, he enjoyed these visits, while they delighted in his nonsensical play on words. He would tell them, for instance, how difficult it was for an actor to lie motionless as dead Caesar when he had a bad cold – 'you see, dears, if he sneezed they would have to call him "Julius Sneezer"!'

Iris's childhood thus unfolded against a background of stage illusions: the fairyland settings for *A Midsummer Night's Dream*, 'a wood near Athens', with live rabbits lolloping and scuttling

---

* Lady Fortescue, *There's Rosemary ... There's Rue* (Blackwood, 1939).
† Diana Cooper, *The Rainbow Comes and Goes* (Hart-Davis, 1958).

1a and b) Iris's parents, Sir Herbert and Lady Tree

2a) Iris as a child

2b) Iris as an art student

2c) Viola Tree

The Buttercup Fields of Childhood

about the stage planted with wild flowers. She began to learn history through Shakespeare's plays; she felt the grandeur that was Rome as she took her first steps through a cardboard forum; and she expected life to provide such magnificence as Henry VIII's banqueting hall at Hampton Court. Her imagination was also nurtured on the many-hued fairy books of Andrew Lang with their romantic illustrations by H. E. Ford.

At an early age she started taking an interest in her physical appearance. The plump, freckled little girl who grinned back at her from the looking-glass had hair the colour and texture of the finest spun sugar ('angel's hair' is the confectioner's term). She knew she was considered the plainest of the three sisters, but comforted herself with the story of the Ugly Duckling and vowed that one day she too would be beautiful.

Lady Granby, who was a close friend of Maud's sister, had a house at Bognor and the Tree girls often joined the Manners children there during the summer. Lady Granby and Maud visited them during weekends, arriving with an escort of fashionable beaux in immaculate white flannel suits and panama hats or jaunty boaters. The two women were elegantly dressed for the beach in wasp-waisted linen skirts which broke into pleats below their knees and swept the shingle as they walked. The texture of their rose-petal skin was protected from sun and wind by finely-tucked white *batiste* blouses with high necks and long leg-of-mutton sleeves. Veils covered their straw hats and were lowered to shade their faces.

Iris was like a Kingsley water-baby. Her nanny, who used to have a stone bottle of Plymouth gin tucked away in the pram, found it impossible to keep her charge on dry land except by tethering her to a rope and fastening the other end around her own stout waist.

Viola, too, was enamoured of the sea, so much so that her father felt constrained to warn her 'not to swim or float too boastfully'. She was his favourite and he watched closely over her developing character in which he saw a reflection of his own. 'Always count up to ten when you are going to be angry,' he advised her. 'I have to count up to fifteen.'

One day, in a fit of temper, she deliberately broke a window.

The Rainbow Picnic

'This, my child, is wickedness,' he said.

'No, father,' she replied, 'this is heredity.'

Maud wanted to bring her up as a little lady 'all sugar-and-spice', but Herbert encouraged her to be a tomboy and, perhaps because he had hoped for a son, was secretly pleased to see her behave like 'a rogue and a vagabond'. He allowed her to stay up late and even took her to the theatre with him, where she sat in his dressing-room and watched as he put on his make-up. When it was time for him to go on stage, the doorman saw her to a hansom cab. She swanked about this to the Manners children, but they merely retorted: 'No lady goes in a hansom alone.'

Meanwhile the two younger sisters continued to share the joys and sorrows of the nursery, presided over by a nanny. To Iris, Felicity appeared a dream of beauty with her dark red hair, attractive little nose and round, blue eyes. But Viola seemed to belong to a higher realm altogether, intrepidly vaulting gates, climbing trees and sliding down the banisters. Her room was like Aladdin's cave, crammed with such treasures as chunks of amethyst, quartz and amber, glass cases containing bird's eggs and butterflies, albums filled with pressed flowers. There was even a cut-out model of a stage with paper figures worked by wires and cardboard scenery designed and painted by herself. She would dress Felicity and Iris as knights – Sir Lancelot and Sir Gawain – arm them with wooden swords and spears, and mount them in turn on her old rocking-horse....

When the time came for the girls to be educated by a governess, none came up to Maud's exacting requirements. A favourite principle of hers, 'Never apologize to children or governesses', inevitably reduced them to martyrs or rebels, and one of them was even heard to murmur: *'Quelle famille de serpents!'* Of the twenty-five successively engaged, Iris loved only one – a Scandinavian whom she nicknamed 'Helga' after a heroine in *The Brown Fairy Book*. She was young and pretty and encouraged the children to run rather than walk, but since Maud considered her 'too modern' she in turn soon left.

Maud then decided to enrol Viola as a student at the Royal Academy of Dramatic Art,* and arranged for Felicity and Iris

* Founded by Herbert Beerbohm Tree in 1904.

The Buttercup Fields of Childhood

to attend the fashionable day school run by Miss Wolff, an excellent and unusual teacher with a method of instruction peculiar to herself. Her classes were held in a private home in South Audley Street, and her pupils sat round tables in the drawing-room, not at desks and not in separate forms.

Iris was one of the youngest girls – too young, it was thought, to take the examination in English literature set for university students. But, having shown such interest during the classes, she was allowed to sit for the paper and astonished everyone by getting the highest marks of all.

It was at this unusual school that she made friends with Nancy, the daughter of Sir Bache and Lady Cunard, a frail, small-boned girl with long thin legs and slender ankles, eyes of sapphire-blue, fine straight hair the colour of pale sunshine, and a vulnerable, slightly receding, dimpled chin. Her delicate appearance, however, masked a steel-like strength of character, and she abided by her determined ideals and fierce loyalty to her friends, as Iris discovered when she went to a tea-party given by her and mockingly referred to one of the other girls as 'niminy-piminy little Miss Banana Curls'. Nancy promptly turned on her: 'How *dare* you make fun of my guest!'

Nevertheless, their mutual affection and esteem survived such outbursts and their friendship was permanently cemented by many interests and passions in common. They both wrote poetry, for instance, and often read their verses to each other, Nancy in a small, clipped, high-pitched voice, Iris with an intonation like a ship's bell heard out at sea.

Another close friend was Jacqueline Alexander, brown-eyed, plump, pert as a robin, and appropriately nicknamed 'Cocky'. She was usually in Miss Wolff's black books for breaking rules and playing practical jokes. Her sense of fun seemed to bubble up from a source of mirth which could not be contained and overflowed when any degree of solemnity was required. She and Iris shared secrets, hatched plots and corresponded with each other in a code of their own devising.

She came to stay in the summer holidays, when the Trees took a house near the sea. Sometimes the two girls made roving expeditions in a pony cart, rattling down Sussex lanes, singing

The Rainbow Picnic

popular songs, trails of eglantine and honeysuckle twisted round their haymakers' hats. Other days they spent on isolated beaches, dancing and singing on the shore. Before leaving their marine picnic ground each of them would cast one stocking into the sea as a votive offering. The governess engaged for the holiday could not understand why they invariably returned wearing only one stocking each. When questioned, they gave absurd answers: 'We had to strangle someone', 'A man wanted a keepsake', 'We gave them to the pony – it was hungry', 'We used them for shrimping'.

The local pastry-cooks provided opportunity for further sport. While one of them engaged the shop assistant in conversation, pretending to deliberate over the choice of cakes, the other would finger the jam tarts, deliberately crumbling the edge of the pastry. Then they would both say, 'We'd like a couple of these, but for the price of one because they're damaged'.

Another life-long friendship formed at Miss Wolff's was with dark-haired, brown-eyed Maud Nelkie, the child of rich parents, who was always beautifully and suitably dressed. She was a very intelligent girl with keen powers of observation and a lively wit which provoked Iris to peals of uncontrollable laughter. (All the Tree girls laughed so heartily that they were sometimes reduced to a state of incontinence.)

Meanwhile, true to the vow she had made as a little girl, Iris continued to take great interest in her physical appearance. Cupping her round face in her long-fingered but rather red hands, she would look at her reflection in the mirror and assess each feature. Her eyes were deep blue and set wide apart; half-closed they looked like twin new moons. Her nose was straight, though not so alluring as Felicity's. Her mouth, she thought, resembled a flower. Her skin was not flawless, but all the more attractive for being dusted with freckles. Her body was too plump, granted, but her breasts were as neat and firm as apples. She began to take pleasure in the artistic, almost fancy-dress clothes that her mother designed following the fashion set by the duchess of Rutland.* She and her two sisters looked like Velasquez infantas in black velvet frocks with sashes of apricot-

* Formerly Lady Granby.

The Buttercup Fields of Childhood

coloured silk which emphasized the russet gold of their hair. Their shot green-and-blue taffeta coats, trimmed with gold braid and worn with Napoleonic hats, were the envy of all their friends.

Tree loved festivals and feast-days and always put on a Christmas entertainment for children. His choice for 1908 was *Pinkie and the Fairies*, written by the painter Graham Robertson.

The theme of this play is a fairy party held by the little people in a pine wood at midnight. They invite Pinkie and her friend Tommy and tell them they will summon any fairy-story character they would like to meet. It is a June night and the moon is full. The grassy slope is planted with ferns; rabbits scuttle around and birds fly among the trees; the flickering light of fireflies is reflected in a pool from which slowly rises a large waterlily bud; the petals unfurl to disclose the fairy queen. . . . Cinderella drives up in a glass coach drawn by six white ponies. . . .

The Sleeping Beauty (played by Viola) appears, in floating draperies of rose and purple. She looks like one of Granville's illustrations for *Les Fleurs Animées*, as she fans herself languidly with an enormous poppy-head and sings a lullaby. . . .

The first performance took the form of a Christmas party given by Felicity and Iris, who were allowed to invite their friends with their parents. Thus, as in Shakespeare, when there is a play within a play, here was a party within a party. After the performance the children went up on the stage, were received by Ellen Terry, met the other members of the cast and drove in Cinderella's coach. Then they all adjourned to the dome where a splendid feast was spread in the banqueting room.

The Trees usually spent part of the Christmas holidays at Belvoir Castle with the Rutlands. The children found the duke and duchess kind but alarming, and enjoyed the freedom of the huge house where they could hide away in attics and towers to whisper their secrets and mock and mimic the duller, conventional guests who sat indoors, tweeded and hatted, making only the briefest sorties for shooting and hunting. Iris felt small, uncouth and ill-clad. She was dazzled by Diana Manners's beauty and intelligence, admiring her conquest of old and young alike.

The Rainbow Picnic

Viola and Marjorie Manners would sing duets together in the gallery or, encouraged by the artistic duchess, take plaster casts of each other's hands, while the younger children made raids on the still-room, drawn there by the smell of baking bread, to wheedle cakes and sweetmeats from the still-room maid. When snow fell they went tobogganing down the steep slopes from where the castle perched.

In 1909 Tree was knighted. At that time he was appearing as Malvolio in *Twelfth Night* and on the evening after he had been dubbed, when he delivered the lines: 'Some are born great, others achieve greatness and some have greatness thrust upon them', the audience held up the performance as they rose to their feet, cheering and applauding for several minutes.

It was in this production that Viola, little more than a child, 'divinely tall and most divinely fair', had her first Shakespearean part, appropriately that of Viola. Her mother would have preferred her to make her début in Society, but was never able to resist the determination of any of her daughters, even when she feared their hearts were set on a dangerous course. Fortunately Viola had sufficient vitality to extract the honey from the comb of both worlds.

She was at her best when acting with her father, for instance as the queen in *Richard II*:

> Each time it seemed as if he were surprised to see me standing there, and as if we were really to say good-bye to each other for the last time. Then I fell on his neck, and said my piece sobbing, because at that moment I was not Richard's Queen but my father's daughter. . . . He never could begin his speech at once – he was so worried by my tears. . . .*

Her spontaneous originality endeared her to the so-called 'Corrupt Coterie', a cabal formed by the Manners girls and the children of that other clique known as 'The Souls'. With a voice that was wild and yet tender she also sang her way into the hearts of Margot Asquith and her sister Lady Ribblesdale, both of whom liked to accompany her on the piano. In due course she thus became a favourite of Herbert Asquith, the Prime

* Viola Tree's appreciation of her father in *Herbert Beerbohm Tree*.

The Buttercup Fields of Childhood

Minister. Theirs was a friendship akin to the affinity that existed in eighteenth-century France between old philosophers and intellectual young women. At one time they wrote to each other daily. She was popular, too, with Lord Ribblesdale, Master of the King's Buckhounds, who lent her horses to ride and called her 'my *coupe d'oubli*'. Such was her success indeed that some of the dowagers presenting less well-favoured daughters in the marriage mart of Mayfair looked down high-bridged noses at her and remarked: 'You can't float about on a wire as Ariel with no petticoats and appear at a ball half an hour later in white satin!'

In 1909 the Trees moved to the house they loved best of all – Walpole House in Chiswick Mall, built by Charles II for his mistress Barbara Villiers, Duchess of Cleveland. The Trees claimed it was used by Thackeray as his model for Miss Pinkerton's academy for young ladies.* Maud, with her unerring taste, made it even more beautiful, but her daughters complained that by installing electric light she drove away the ghost of Barbara Villiers, who was believed to haunt the place, her heels tapping up and down the staircase as she wrung her hands and bemoaned her beauty marred by smallpox.

In these romantic surroundings Iris approached the threshold of adolescence, retaining all her childlike qualities and at the same time developing a certain artistic and even social precocity. At the age of twelve, at one of the *al fresco* parties for which the Trees were justly renowned, she was heard to remark: 'Mother, you can't serve cod *and* salmon.'

Meanwhile she continued to write poetry and showed some of her verses to Viola, who found them as fresh and flowerlike as her little sister's name and even roused Mr Asquith's interest in them. 'You have forgotten to send me the irises,' he complained in one of his letters.

She also took to drawing, in which she showed the same quality of freshness and delicacy; her work was full of movement, sometimes tragic but mostly comic, for she seemed to

---

* A house in Burlington Lane, Chiswick, next to the George and Devonshire pub, bears the official blue plaque identifying it as the house in question.

have inherited some of the talent and whimsical wit of her Uncle Max, who was a frequent visitor at Walpole House.

One day he found her and Felicity engaged in printing the names of roses on little wooden tags which were to be hung on the respective bushes: *Cuisse de nymphe émue, Gloire de Dijon, Maiden's Blush, Clara Butt, Princess of Wales, Albertine.* . . . The girls were briefly called away from their task and on their return found their uncle had replaced their labels with a set of his own: *Crippen, Ethel le Neve, La Voisin, Jack the Ripper, Charlie Peace, Madame Steinheil,* etc. . . .

In 1912 Viola abandoned the stage in the hope of becoming an opera singer. Her mother and friends assured her that the charm of her voice lay in its untamed, pagan quality. But she was determined to have it properly trained and, despite their pleas, made arrangements to study with a teacher in Milan.

This decision was also prompted by an ulterior motive. She was deeply in love with a young man called Alan Parsons, whom she had first seen walking along the breakwater at Brancaster, where the Trees were staying for the summer. She had been bowled over by his dark Italian Renaissance style of beauty, allied, as she presently discovered, to a scholarly mind. He was the son of the Rector of Tandridge in Surrey, had been a King's Scholar at Eton, and had obtained a First in Mods and a Second in English at Oxford. Maud liked and admired him but, hoping that Viola would make a spectacular marriage, disapproved of him as a prospective husband for her. Faced with parental opposition, the young lovers therefore became secretly engaged and, for some reason which she could scarcely explain even to herself, Viola felt that her troth would be more firmly plighted by a period of exile abroad.

In Milan she was joined by an Austrian friend, Maria Schwelter, a promising young pianist eager to become a professional. At first the two girls lodged with a family but, after learning sufficient Italian to fend for themselves, soon found themselves in need of greater independence and longed for quarters of their own. True daughter of her father, Viola promptly raised the wind by pawning her jewels for £50, which enabled them to buy a dilapidated little house, furnish it with second-hand junk, and engage a peasant girl called Speranza for the housework.

It was a struggle to keep within their meagre allowances, but spaghetti and white Asti cost little and they were both willing to make sacrifices to pay for their respective lessons. In her eagerness Viola over-exerted herself by engaging a second teacher unbeknown to the first and thus subjecting her voice to twice the strain. At times, whenever she had an audition it took fright and vanished. And so additional expenses were incurred in order to restore it with the help of a doctor and throat specialist.

Life in the little house took on a new *brio* with the arrival of Iris, whom her parents had allowed to join her sister in order to study music and drawing. Fifteen years old, she was like a palomino foal, eager for pastures new, excited by foreign climes, intoxicated by a greater degree of freedom than she had hitherto known. Gregarious as ever, she made friends wherever she went. Even more high-spirited than before, she sang and danced round the house. Viola's teacher was impressed by her voice, which Iris herself described as 'strongish and like the beast before he turns into a prince', but realized after giving her a few lessons that she would never have the patience to train it.

Shortly afterwards Viola was engaged to sing the part of Salomé in a provincial opera house, with Maria as her accompanist. So as not to leave Iris alone in their absence they arranged for her to stay with Maria's music mistress but asked her to be sure to call at the little house regularly to see that all was well.

Iris revelled in her independence and wrote to Maud Nelkie:

I am rather a success here; my hair is admired and every kind of bulk is adored. I got a love letter from a fat German the other day who 'could not forget my hair and innocent face. . . .'

I am trying to keep as pure as possible but it's rather difficult. I am in love with a beautiful Italian called Ludovici who gives me lessons in the language on a crimson sofa. His hair is as near blue-black as Stephen's ink, eyes as brown as the velvet I adore and a mouth as good as mine when little and

The Rainbow Picnic

a complexion as from the pomegranates on the walls of Jerusalem.

And a few weeks later:

I am having a glorious time, living a somewhat bohemian life and eating bohemian spaghetti.

Don't you think the Duomo Cathedral is the most beautiful place in the world, inside, and next to it don't you think I am the most wonderful thing?

I hope I shall come back here; when one sees a direct line one wants to start off for it and not turn away to the other little paths. I want to do so many things and of course I shall end by doing nothing. Women never do anything except spoil the lives of men – that is their only consolation.

Meanwhile Viola heard that Iris was neglecting to carry out the instructions she had left with her and wrote an admonishing letter:

Dearest Iris,

I think you are pretty selfish to go on your own pleasures, and not to go home sometimes and see that Speranza is all right. She has absolutely no money, and I left three cheques for you in the yellow box. Also Speranza ought to go with you to Borgo Nuovo, to tidy up your things as Madame B. has only one servant. At least she can do that. Twice a day she ought to come – to dress you in the morning, and put your things away in the evening. You must know that I am too busy and too far away. If you had gone yourself you would have found the paints at once. Speranza does not know 'greasepaint' – how should she? They are in a box with my sandals and the gold powder for my hair, all together – Maria says, in the green or yellow box upstairs so don't muddle it up. I can get along without them perhaps until you come. Apparently there will be only three representations.

The whole thing is not much worth while I fear, except as rehearsal for the future, and you must decide whether it is worth while to come. You mustn't travel with Speranza; it's too expensive, and there's no necessity. You have not to

The Buttercup Fields of Childhood

change and can travel on that twelve o'clock with a friendly lady. I think Tuesday will be the last representation. As it is, the impresario is so poor I am playing the first and second violins myself. Maria is playing the piano in the orchestra.

Viola's next engagement was to sing the leading part in *Orpheus in the Underworld*, under the direction of her father. And so with Iris, Maria and Speranza, she returned to England after rustling up enough money for their third-class tickets.

Iris's childhood now lay behind her: a landscape of hallowed memories to which she returned in reverie for the rest of her life. Unalloyed happiness had been provided by loving and beloved parents who had made a point of following the formula for bringing up children which Maud herself had once voiced when interviewed by a reporter: 'Make them remember their childhood with pleasure.'

3 Student at the Slade

On returning to England Viola found there was no longer any opposition to her marrying Alan Parsons, and so, when the run of *Orpheus in the Underworld* came to an end, she abandoned her singing career and set about making plans for a July wedding at St Martin's-in-the-Fields.

Her wedding dress, modelled on the one worn by the Empress Marie-Louise when she married Napoleon, was designed by Diana Manners. As she drove to the church with her father, he surprised her by asking: 'Do you like Alan, dear?' – a question which at this stage she considered somewhat superfluous – and as they drew near His Majesty's, he turned to her and said: 'I'm just going to pop in for a moment, dear.' And so she sat outside, watching his beloved figure – flamboyant coat-tails, hat, stick and all – vanish through the swing doors only to return a few minutes later having found out that all was well.

By this time the Trees had moved from Chiswick to a corner house in All Souls Place. Several pantechnicons from Harrods had been required to transfer all the furniture, which prompted Maud to remark: 'We seem to be out-Harroding Harrod.' Iris disliked the new house, which she described as 'looking like a slice of cake', and missed the Chiswick garden and riverside, but her sadness was mitigated by the prospect of enrolling as a student at the Slade School of Art. Meanwhile she bore a close resemblance to 'the nimble fiend' of Raymond Asquith's poem *In Praise of Young Girls*, who

> Has raised a laugh against her bosom friend,
> Melted a Marquis, mollified a Jew,
> Kissed every member of the Eton crew,
> Ogled a bishop, quizzed an ancient peer,
> Has danced a tango and has dropped a tear,
> Fresh from the schoolroom, pink and plump and pert,
> Bedizened, bouncing, artful and alert.

Like her elder sisters, she too now began to realize how much her mother suffered from her father's romantic philandering, but she also understood that a spirit like his could not be curbed. 'What can we do to make mother's life more lovely?' Viola wrote to her, after Maud had confided how painful it was to give a heart-felt performance in a love scene with Herbert when she felt as though she was wearing someone else's clothes.

Maud was compensated to a certain extent when the handsome actor, Lewis Waller, fell in love with her. But there was a sharp edge to the situation, for he was one of the finest actors in Tree's Shakespearean company – he had played Brutus in *Julius Caesar* to Tree's Mark Antony, with Maud in the part of Lucius, the bare-foot slave-boy who sings and plays the lute to him in the orchard scene – and his performance was so brilliant that he sometimes received a greater ovation than Tree himself. (His many female admirers wore buttons inscribed with the letters 'K.O.W.', standing for 'Keen On Waller'.) Maud was too high-principled to allow herself to embark on a passionate relationship with him, particularly since he was married, but she appreciated his devotion and, in his sympathetic company, forgot her sadness and recovered her self-confidence; her wit crackled and her eyes sparkled again.

One day, however, while driving with him in his motor-car, they had an accident in which her jaw was broken so badly that her looks were permanently impaired. This tragedy not only put an end to her career as a leading lady but affected her all the more deeply since she had made a life-long cult of beauty and considered the slightest disfigurement well-nigh unbearable. She derived some consolation from Herbert's renewed compassion and gentleness – from then on he did his best to shield her from any hurt his philandering might cause – and in due course she even brought herself to joke about his peccadilloes: 'Herbert's love-affairs begin with a compliment and end with a confinement,' she lightly remarked; and when someone laughingly suggested she should train their dog to bark at every woman Herbert courted, she replied: 'Our last one did exactly that, but alas died from lack of sleep!'

In order to give her a new interest, Herbert took a short lease on Wyndham's Theatre and let her manage it. She produced two plays there but both were failures; Herbert lost the £3,000 he had invested and she, ironically, was left with just enough money to buy a motor-car of her own.

After this venture she threw all her creative energy into restoring an old barn which Herbert bought for her. It stood on the banks of the river at Sutton Courtenay and faced a former coal-wharf and was therefore blackened by coal-dust as well as being roofless and floorless. 'I must say I don't think much of it,' Herbert wrote to Viola, 'but I expect your mother will make something of it.' And indeed she did, transforming it into a river paradise for the children, who spent many a golden summer day there collecting tadpoles and water-boatmen in jam jars, tickling trout and fishing from an old boat.

The idyll was abruptly interrupted when Margot Asquith appeared like a wicked fairy to repair what Maud called 'a temporary black-out in our friendship'. But far from sealing the rift, the visitor promptly widened it by offering unsolicited advice on how to improve the property: 'Buy up the adjoining land, the public house in front, the private house next door, the cottages on the other side. Pull down that hideous hut, flood the garden, knock down the wall and dam the river.'

Understandably nettled, Maud retorted: 'Since you're so clever, why not buy the place and do it yourself? I'm willing to sell.' To her surprise Margot Asquith agreed.

Subsequently the Trees rented a succession of country houses, each of which Maud chose in order to indulge her passion for redecorating and providing an attractive setting for her family.

Student at the Slade

Thus they took Glottenham at Robertsbridge because its enormous rooms and galleries seemed to her a perfect background for the beautiful golden garlands that had been hung on the walls of His Majesty's for the Shakespearean coronation festival; but by the time they moved in, these had been sold. For many summers they also rented a seaside house in Sussex from the William Nicholsons, who lived next door. The neighbourly feuds which occurred were aggravated by Iris falling off her horse over a fence into the Nicholsons' garden.

In 1913 Iris was briefly banished from London and sent to Glottenham to stay with 'a sad married cousin' who was asked by Maud 'to exert her influence for the good'. This infuriated her and she wrote to Maud Nelkie:

> Please forgive me for Mother's impish, comicish brutality – and all her cowardly wrong-headedness. . . . I am sitting with a headache on the banks of a drain by the side of a highroad among the hop-pickers. Mother came down and refused to let me go because I was 'restless'.

Maud Nelkie also came down to Glottenham for the weekend. She was being launched into the life of a fashionable débutante and had been fitted out with a wardrobe of expensive clothes suitable for the London season, which Iris half envied and half despised.

'How did you like Glottenham?' she wrote to her after her visit.

> A ragged place but it laughed up its sleeve at your trim turn-out because it has the soul of freedom (a soul all paupers and bores choose to excuse their unpopularity).

During this period of rebellion, as an act of defiance and Grand Guignol exhibitionism, Iris cut off her plait of Rhinegold tresses while travelling in a train and left it behind her on the seat. She was thus one of the first girls in England to appear with bobbed hair.

Shortly afterwards Maud rented a derelict house in France. 'It will be good for the children to learn French fishing on the banks of the Seine,' she explained to Herbert. 'Insane!' he

...ut she took it all the same. She was then acting in
...y, so that the only way in which she could make the
...itable was to cross the Channel every Saturday night
... evening performance, spend Sunday there and return
... ...ay in time for the play.

It was in this French riverside house, under the cloudless blue skies of the summer of 1913, that Maud and her daughters spent what she described as 'a white muslin summer' and where Herbert in due course joined them, radiant after his annual cure at Marienbad. 'Do come here,' Iris wrote to Maud Nelkie, 'and drink flame-coloured cider and eat wild strawberries and cream-cheese; such a lovely uncomfortable house, such a long river to bathe in; such willows to entangle one; so many ripening apples and barley-sheaves.' It was here, again, that they were staying when war was declared in the following year. In the rush to get back to England Maud somehow got separated from the rest of the family and was stranded at Dieppe. When at last she reached England she found Herbert waiting for her at Victoria, having met a succession of trains, and her sinking heart was straight away buoyed up by his genuine anxiety and solicitude.

In spite of the war, Iris continued to attend classes at the Slade. She admitted to Maud Nelkie that she went out of her way to appear *outrée* among her fellow students, and indeed her originality was soon remarked. She was still much too plump for her liking but, with her youth and height, such voluptuousness became her well and her mother-of-pearl flesh tones reflected light like those of a Renoir model. She blushed easily, but only her closest friends realized she was shy since she adopted the defensive camouflage of a swinging gait and head held challengingly high. Her manner of speech closely resembled her father's, her lovely hands gesturing as though pulling threads out of the air and weaving a tapestry of words. When her emotions were aroused in argument, she seemed armed with an invisible épée, thrusting and parrying like a duellist as she made her point.

One of her closest friends at the Slade was Dora Carrington, with whom she carried on a regular correspondence during the holidays. When Iris told her that in character she resembled a

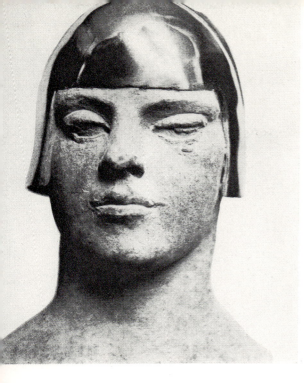

3a) Epstein bust of Iris

3b) Portrait of Iris by Dora Carrington

4) Sybil Hart-Davis

box of mixed biscuits, she replied: 'I shall marry Huntley and Palmers' son and have a biscuit engraved on top of my notepaper.' Meanwhile she wrote on paper engraved with the figure of a girl carrying on her back a large sack inscribed '1 ton'.

Iris's paper, on the other hand, was yellow, with a stylized yellow tree (symbolic of her surname) engraved over the address. 'Does it turn green in summer?' Carrington enquired.

Iris's fellow-students were surprised by the handsome, elegantly dressed young men, top-hatted, grey-gloved and carrying walking-sticks, who came to take her out to tea at Gunters; but her parents were alarmed by her growing independence, fussed over her unpredictable comings and goings and were curious to know the company she kept.

In order to have a bolt-hole free from parental surveillance, she and Nancy Cunard secretly rented a studio in which they kept a store of theatrical make-up – sticks of grease-paint, pots of gold-dust, rouge (applied with a hare's foot), Reckitt's blue powder for their eyelids, to intensify the colour of their eyes – and a wardrobe of motley for fancy dress parties, including one of Sir Bache Cunard's top hats. In this refuge they met their friends, gave clandestine feasts and talked through the night by the light of guttering candles, reading poetry aloud and smoking cigarettes. At dawn they would steal home armed with well-fabricated alibis.

One morning, returning in fancy dress from an Albert Hall ball, they plunged into the Serpentine and emerged with bedraggled feathers, dripping chiffon and spangles, to find themselves confronted with a policeman who took their names and addresses and brought a charge against them. Their parents then confiscated their latch-keys and imposed a curfew. The existence of the studio remained secret, however, and with the forging of new keys they were able to continue their clandestine life.

Forbidden playgrounds were investigated. They ate eggs and bacon in cabmen's shelters, avoiding the one in Piccadilly known as 'The Junior Turf Club' where Sir Herbert sometimes stayed until six o'clock in the morning drinking coffee and playing dominoes with the cabbies. They drank beer in public houses and wine at the Café Royal. Restaurants were a new experience and the foreign ones in Soho were their favourites.

At the Cavendish Hotel they were made welcome by Mrs Rosa Lewis who knew Iris was popular with her hero, Lord Ribblesdale. 'I know all about you – and young Viola. You're Barebum Tree's daughter. You don't have to pay for anything in my place, have some champagne.' And so some rich client would find mysterious bottles of Veuve Clicquot added to his bill.

Iris had been brought up to love dogs, and there had always been one in the family. Each had had his own particular song, chosen by Maud, and sung to him in chorus. This custom had originated with 'Bully Boy', a bandy-legged old bulldog who had appeared with Herbert in *The Dancing Girl*. His song was *Gilbert the Filbert* and he would listen with his head cocked on one side as the Trees sang:

> 'E's the pride of Piccadilly
> 'E's the pink of Pall Mall.

This was before Iris was born, but 'Bully Boy' had always been a legend to her and when she was allowed to have a dog of her own she chose a bull-terrier of the 'wild' strain, the kind of dog that is often depicted in Georgian prints snarling at the heels of a Regency rake or a member of the Mohawk Club. 'Churgin', as she called him, possessed all the fighting blood and aggressive instincts of his ancestors who were bred to bait bulls and bears in the ring and seize the throat of a canine opponent in a death-dealing grip; and the swains who visited her and Nancy in their secret hideout must have found him an ugly customer, as he stood snarling at the foot of the stairs and fixing them with his baleful pink-rimmed eyes.

Iris described her appearance, character and life at this time in a vivid word picture:

> I was born in 1897
> I have a fringe –
> I have whiskers –
> I have a studio in
> Fitzroy Street, red and

Student at the Slade

white floor in checks,
black velvet sofa
black velvet blinds,
blue cups and plates
red rimmed looking
glass red table –
Mother nor Daddy
know of it, *unberufen*,
I have a white dress
with black velvet
masks dangling from
ribbons upon it.
I have a red dress
red as a pillar box
laced up with bright
green ribbons and bright
blue – they are four
yards long and
go twice round my
hips criss-cross –
I have red shoes
and a red hat.
I shall have a pale blue
bedroom with pink
windows –
I have had 28
lovers, some more
some less –
I have Greek feet.
I have a fierce
bull-terrier –
I have a hat brim
worn without a crown –
I drink absinthe.
I borrow money.
I have loved men
I have loved women.
I am a jolly laide –

The Rainbow Picnic

> I paint my eye
> lashes gold, they are
> already gold –
> I am fat.
> I am a soul.
> I am an artist.
> I am a wanton.
> I am a hypocrite.

Many portraits were painted of her at this period of her life. She sat simultaneously to Vanessa Bell and Duncan Grant, who had neighbouring studios, also to Roger Fry (who complained of her unpunctuality), Epstein, Guevara and Augustus John. Carrington, too, portrayed her – in an exquisite little picture executed in coloured tinsel paper under glass – against a star-dotted sky, mounted like Joan of Arc on a white horse, with a blue cloak hanging from her shoulders.* She wore dresses made from woollen and linen textile woven in the Omega workshop and designed by Duncan Grant and Vanessa Bell, who wrote asking her to be photographed in one of their garments 'to send out in a polite letter to our customers'.

She had met Augustus John when she was seventeen, at one of Lady Ottoline Morell's Thursdays, a milieu in which she felt more at ease than at smart parties. She was wearing a dress of her own design laced with blue and green ribbons, one blue stocking and one green, and the famous hat brim without a crown. There were others equally eccentrically garbed.

At Ottoline's there were all kinds of dress-ups. Her rooms were scented with pomanders, pot-pourri and packed with genii in full cry. Bleats and squeaks of eccentric speech. John's basso profundo muttering rare but penetrating sentences. He spoke melodiously a beautiful Bardic almost Biblical English, slightly roughened by countryfied intonations.

At first meeting I experienced an immediate intimacy as if I was part of his landscape which has remained in my vision ever since. It has rounded hills, pale or slate-blue skies, grey rocks. Its people were angels dressed as peasants, women who

* See plate 3b.

baked crusty bread which wafted a hungry fragrance that called the labourers home. There was lavender in the coarse linen and brown or blue jugs of thick cream. Jars of wine were served under their vines to scowling men who drank into the night of love-making, singing, dancing.

But there's another point more difficult to define except romantically for it was essentially romantic.

I pursued these visions into real life and expected too much of them. Groups of villagers by well or fountain, drying sheets and waving shirts, would be my comrades and their beasts would come mooing home to me.*

Not only did she feel she belonged to John's landscapes, she was later actually immortalized in one of them: a large mural in which she is depicted among a crowd of Belgian refugees fleeing from Louvain during the First World War, her fair fringed head bending over a babe cradled in her arms.†

'I love your freckles and blue shadows,' John told her when she was sitting for him, and he wrote a poem to her which ended with the lines:

> With that old strange allure
> Voluptuously virginal and passionately pure.

By this time Iris had met Sybil Hart-Davis, Duff Cooper's sister, a married woman about ten years older than herself who, though moving in less Bohemian circles, soon became a close friend and trusted confidante. The letters they exchanged illustrate the contrast in their natures and the difference in their lives. Here, for instance, is a self-portrait of Sybil on the eve of a visit abroad:

> I have got a jolly bathing dress, it looks like a dock leaf in the water, wonderful green silk and a dear little hat to wear in Venice.
>
> I smoke too much and am all fluttery. My nails are beautifully manicured and my underclothes have improved a bit, lace and billowing pale pink silks, also dozens of new white

* From an unpublished essay, *In Praise of Augustus John*, by Iris Tree.
† Mural at Paul Channon's house, Cheyne Walk.

The Rainbow Picnic

> silk stockings, to say nothing of green and gold brocade shoes with enormous diamonds on them.
>
> I have not seen a Greek book since I last saw you.
>
> I talked tête à tête to Raymond* last Monday morning from 10 till 1.30. I was *thrilled* at the time and just after: but all things lose their glamour and dwindle.

And here, a description of her mood on returning to her home in England:

> Why don't you write to me at least twice a day?
>
> Here I am all alone watching the last leaves fall: a stranger to drink and fashion.
>
> Bless you for sending the song to old Rich.†
>
> Send me a song I can sing to the icy brown waves that beat on this barren shore; or a poem that I can murmur to myself at nights when the wind shakes the rafters, and ghosts sick with ennui pace the panelled passages.
>
> Have you forgotten how short and gold my hair is, how slight my body and great my charm?
>
> Write me an endless letter quickly.

Sybil's handwriting was small, delicate and clear – unlike Iris's, as she pointed out:

> Your writing is not only unpleasing to the eye but totally illegible, my sweet, so I don't think you will ever get this letter owing to the address being quite unreadable. However I write with the faint hope that owing to your peculiar appearance you may have become sufficiently celebrated for addresses to be superfluous. I really do wish your writing was not so ignoble.

In lighter vein, from a country house party:

> So you have deserted my pale wavering banner: in a word joined the great majority. Never mind, a sweet dignity hangs about the forsaken especially when they are bowed but not

---

* Raymond Asquith.
† Her husband, Richard Hart-Davis.

bloody. . . . The world is all grey today and I have been forced to listen to music unceasingly. . . . My beloved little decadent friend, it seems too long since I saw you. May I come to Glotts next Sunday perhaps and lie in the nettles?

This is not a proper letter you may say, but you are such a snob I thought you would like a letter decorated with a coronet.

And again, from Kirkdale Manor in Yorkshire:

I tread on millions of dead grouse to eat, a luffly (*sic*) house. Wonderful long-tailed Arab ponies to ride on purple moors. Members of parliament who hang on my words. Every evening I win little piles of sovereigns at bridge with F. E. Smith and the sun is shining and yet 'tired with all this' for you, ill mannered, freckled and much too fat, I yearn.

Meanwhile, through Augustus John, Iris had met Horace de Vere Cole, the well-known practical joker whose romantic-sounding name attracted her no less than his exceptionally handsome physique. That such an experienced and dashing man should pay attention to her was a feather in her cap – a feather that could not be flaunted in front of her parents – and so she would creep out like a footpad at night to go adventuring with him. Sometimes, in the early hours, they used to break into pubs and provide themselves with breakfast. She enjoyed the sensation of their being comrades-in-crime and, as she boasted to Sybil, 'I have become the oath on Horace de Vere Cole's lips'.

Her behaviour was very different from that of her sister Felicity, whose tastes were inclined towards hunting and Hurlingham rather than art and romance and whose young men were sportsmen and soldiers as opposed to poets and painters. Where they did see eye to eye, however, was over their cousin, Evelyn Beerbohm, whom they both admired on account of his good looks and general excellence: he drove a four-in-hand, went well out hunting and rode in steeplechases. He even caused a certain rivalry between them, and a pang of jealousy in Iris, who wrote to Sybil complaining:

The Rainbow Picnic

> Why this love of golf? Felicity is playing with Evelyn, round after round. . . . Our cousin seems to be liking her a good deal which is inartistic and irritating of him. Of course if no one liked me at all I should fall completely to pieces, become vulgar, bashful, intense, oozing sentimentality. But people do like me, so I am witty, charming, tactful and full of character. . . . I think it ghastly of you not to write to me, but of course your household duties must occupy your mind.

But a few weeks later she was cock-a-hoop:

> I went to tea with Evelyn who was in bed, too beautifully dressed. How I love men. We played poker which was fun, and dozens of bounders came in and joined the game.

With her youthful years lying like a field of golden buttercups behind her, Iris had so far known little of sorrow; bouts of melancholy had even brought their own poetic pleasure. But now, out of a clear sky, grief struck like a hawk. At a river party given by Constantine Benckendorff, the son of the Russian Ambassador, to which she had been invited with other members of the 'Corrupt Coterie', their daredevil friend, Dennis Anson, dived overboard for fun. Though a strong swimmer he was caught in a treacherous current and swept away. Benckendorff and one of the musicians immediately went to his rescue, but they were soon in difficulties and Benckendorff alone was eventually picked up, in a state of exhaustion.*

Then, in 1914, came the war and one after another more friends fell in battle. Julian and Billy Grenfell, Raymond Asquith, Edward Horner, Patrick Shaw-Stewart and Charles Lister had all seemed like young gods in Iris's eyes and their deaths made her familiar with grief. She derived some consolation, however, from the company of Scatters Wilson,† Lord Ribblesdale's handsome and rakish son-in-law, who, while waiting with his regiment to go to Gallipoli, wrote to her daily and

---

* This incident has been more fully described in *The Rainbow Comes and Goes* by Diana Cooper.
† Sir Matthew Wilson.

asked her 'to dine and do a play' whenever he came to London.

He had a horse which he called Iris Queen and kept in Lord Ribblesdale's stable ready for her to ride. 'But promise me you won't become my mother-in-law,' he begged. Like many others, he regarded the war as 'a jolly adventure. . . . The men and myself are like a lot of schoolboys going off for the holidays. We are all so anxious to get abroad. It will be great fun and keep us busy till peace is declared.'

When he did eventually go overseas (from which he returned safe and sound) it was with a photograph of Iris worn in a locket hung round his neck.

'Have you written any poetry?' Dora Carrington meanwhile wrote to her. 'You ought to be inspired by this war. . . . Astound the world by a ballad. But then you are so lazy. . . . Have all your lovers gone to the "Cruel War in High Germany"? My brothers have gone. But I am annoyed, mostly because I couldn't go to North Wales with John and Ruth and had to come home. But bathing here is good and I lie for long duration of time on top of the sea, called by the vulgar "floating", and draw big red rocks.'

In spite of the war, Iris's link with Bloomsbury held firm and she advised Sybil to 'mix with the modern art clan. They will improve your brains. Clive Bell and Bertrand Russell and Maynard Keynes — all perhaps unattractive but far more intelligent than the rest of London. . . . Another good thing about mingling with ungainly high-brows is that you are at least free and need not bother with kissing since most of them are b————s.'

Her own relationship with Clive Bell was, for a short time, very close; she called him 'Thistledown' and they wrote to each other frequently. In March 1915, from All Souls Place, she wrote:

> Do not neglect the Chelsea Embankment; you may see myself and John blown there with the dissolute leaves in a savage wind — black-hatted and black-kerchiefed — and you may see a streak of orange light across the sky, a tangerine plume nodding over the river to remind you with a pang of my sulphur head, the highlights in my fringe.

The Rainbow Picnic

Three weeks later she wrote from Glottenham:

> You are a very foolish man to have neglected the steely swordplay of my glances and the passionate pressure of my hands. Years come, years go, centuries glorify and undo each other, but rarely do they club together and make perfection from their good and their bad.
>
> Were ever lust and languor, passivity and passion so admirably mingled as in me?
>
> Were ever ignorance and wisdom in league, beauty and ugliness, soul and body as one as they are in your humble?
>
> The only thing I lack is daintyness and then by a certain slimness of the heel and twist of the neck it can be rendered if it is needed.
>
> I am made up of contradictions (as you say) but am therefore one long sally of repartees.
>
> You are God's jester, fallen out of Heaven to wear the devil's livery. Cap and bells, red-shirted blue-stocking! Who can describe you as I?
>
> R.S.V.P.

And so he did, on 1 April 1915, in a vein of fantasy that matched her own:

> All night long I dream't of a young woman in a short tunic and flesh coloured tights and waking cried 'It's All Fools' Day, I must write to Miss Iris.' So I hopped out of bed, tore off my blue and white pyjamas, and donned that pie-bald suit and tinkling cap that I keep to impress one class of young women, just as I keep an Ll.D gown to impress another. But in my dream the lady had turned into a poodle who wouldn't learn to dance; and I doubted what this might portend, and cast about for a solution, and consulted the oracles and Lytton Strachey. And so I began to wonder what you were about, and came to the conclusion that, having gone into the country to pretend that it was spring, you would be in an extremely bad humour to find that it was winter; and I dare say all your [word illegible] have gone sliding.
>
> I don't care for the name of your house, and I very much

Student at the Slade

doubt whether there is such a place as Robertsbridge, but I like your tow-coloured hair and your white skin and your flighty impertinent brain, and your poems, when they are about me. . . . Mid-day: my bells begin to jangle, my head swims: the joke's up: It's not a poodle after all. Bless thee Bottom: thou art translated.

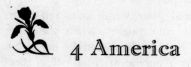

4 America

Late in 1915 Herbert Tree was commissioned by the Triangle Film Company in California to make a serial film of *Macbeth* with himself in the leading part and Constance Collier as Lady Macbeth. He decided to take Iris with him and she persuaded Augustus John to provide a home in the country for her bull-terrier. 'I have given my dog to John whose beard is now torn to wisps and whose mistresses are tattooed with teeth marks,' she wrote to Sybil. Meanwhile her father insisted on her being told (by Lady Tree, since he was too shy to undertake the task himself) that he had two natural sons in America. This revelation in no way disturbed her and she was merely amused when one of her half-brothers met them on the quay at New York and her father introduced him to her saying, 'Be nice to your cousin, dear'.

On the outskirts of Los Angeles they moved into a bungalow equipped with two English servants and a Japanese cook. Orange and lemon trees and a flowering eucalyptus grew in the garden. Father and daughter were like two excited children revelling in the novelty of their surroundings. He allotted her the best bedroom but, noticing the wistful looks he cast towards it, she persuaded him without much difficulty to change rooms.

He enjoyed doing little jobs about the house and using new-fangled gadgets for opening bottles and tins. 'You see, dear, I know all about these things,' he would proudly murmur, and when one of 'these things' failed to function, he merely said, 'Ah, a very good patent non-opener'.

They spent Christmas Day at the Grand Canyon, marvelling at the extraordinary dramatic effects produced by nature: snow fell and was followed by veils of white mist which rose from the ground creating a perfect transformation scene; then, after an interval of five minutes, the sun raised the curtain and three rainbows spanned the horizon. They went for long rides together in the hills, he in the wooden property saddle constructed for *Macbeth*, she following behind like his page.

They amused themselves playing endless games of their own inventing: quarrelling in cockney or pretending to be ordinary people and trying to talk only in clichés. When he ran dry he would explain: 'It's no good, dear, I cannot help being exceptional.' They grew very close to each other during this time and she discovered hitherto unrevealed facets of his nature. He told her that as a schoolboy in Germany he had been so strongly attracted by gipsies and gipsy music that he could never bring himself to visit a Romany encampment for fear of being unable to drag himself away again.

Apart from his film work, while Iris continued to write poetry, he started work on a book of short stories, subsequently entitled *Nothing Matters*. He also seized every opportunity to enlist American sympathy for the Allies, addressing audiences from public platforms, the stage and, on Easter Sunday, from a church pulpit. 'Daddy becomes more and more an extempore artist and makes brilliant speeches each night unprepared,' Iris reported.

Constance Collier was one of Tree's favourite actresses; intuitive of his moods and requirements, she immediately understood when he told her to play a part 'in a mauve voice'. Iris also appreciated her company and promised to be there when she arranged for Tree to meet a friend of hers, the brilliant young comedian Charles Chaplin, but at the last moment Constance was prevented from attending the dinner. Chaplin therefore found himself alone with Tree, and so overawed that he was hardly able to speak. His nervousness increased when Iris appeared, a model of what he considered 'Mayfair sophistication': tall, attractive and no longer plump, entering with her characteristic swagger and carrying a long cigarette holder. 'How do you do, Mr Chaplin,' she said in her deep sonorous voice. 'I suppose I am the only person in the world who has not seen you on the screen.'

Throughout the meal he continued to be tongue-tied until suddenly, all at once, the words were released in a flood:

> Look, Sir Herbert, my success was so sudden that I have had little time to catch up with it. But as a boy of fourteen I saw you as Svengali, as Fagin, as Antony, as Falstaff, some of them many times, and ever since you have been my idol. I never thought of you existing off stage. You were a legend. And to be dining with you tonight in Los Angeles overwhelms me.*

Tree was deeply moved. From then on Chaplin became a close friend of his and, to Iris, an ally who shared many of her tastes. 'We have a common bond, very common, against Daddy: our passion for restaurants, noise, wine, bounders, coons.'†

Macbeth proved to be a financial success and was enthusiastically received by the critics, by the public, by everyone in fact except, apparently, Tree himself who on the opening night was observed fast asleep in his seat.

Now that his film commitment was over, he was able to revert to the stage and embarked on a series of productions, starting with *Oliver Twist*, performed for the benefit of Red Cross funds, with Chaplin as the Artful Dodger. This was followed by *Henry VIII*, which astonished New York on account of the magnificence of the scenery, which was from the London production, specially shipped over from England. The play could have drawn packed houses for months, but long runs were never Tree's habit. He took it off at the peak of its success and put on *The Merchant of Venice*, then *The Merry Wives of Windsor*, justifiably believing that Shakespeare would arouse popular feelings in favour of the Allies.

* Charles Chaplin, *My Autobiography* (Bodley Head, 1964).
† Letter to Sybil Hart-Davis.

Unhappily he allowed himself to be involved in another film, *The Old Folks at Home*, in which he was miscast as an ageing American senator-cum-farmer 'with the Old Testament in one hand and the ace of clubs up my sleeve'. After this embarrassing experience he felt totally disenchanted with film-making and, preferring 'more space and less pace', arranged an autumn Shakespearean tour, starting in Boston.

There he met a remarkable young woman named Solita Solano, who, at the age of twenty-five, was already dramatic critic of *The Boston Herald Traveler* – the first woman to hold such a job on a metropolitan newspaper. Her brown hair was worn short and fell over her forehead in a dark silky wing; her enormous blue-green eyes were quick to observe everything from an etymological conundrum to the *joie de vivre* of an evening; she spoke in a quiet voice which in excitement broke into a little gasp of indrawn breath; her tip-tilted nose had delicately flared nostrils and her mouth combined sensitivity with voluptuousness. Tree was only too willing to accord her an interview in the sitting-room of his suite in the Copley Plaza Hotel.

At the end of it, he told her he would like her to meet his daughter who was occupying the room adjoining. He knocked at the door and Iris's voice answered, 'I'm in bed but come in'. It was five o'clock in the afternoon and she was resting, her face pale against the red-gold of her bobbed hair fanning out over the pillow. 'Finished my poem,' she said, handing her father a sheet of paper which he perused with a smile of pleasure before passing it on to Solita. She found it charming, naïve and fresh – all about the names of precious stones and a bag full of coloured glass – and spontaneously said: 'If you will allow me, I'll print it in my column tomorrow.'

'Oh do, my dear! Lovely!' Tree cried, more excited about this offer than by his own interview.

From then on they saw a lot of each other. He enjoyed showing her off at parties, presenting her with a proud flourish like a conjuror producing a rabbit from a top-hat, and, since she liked and admired him, she returned the affection he soon declared. Sometimes they would walk the streets all night together and dawn would find them still exchanging confidences as they

The Rainbow Picnic

breakfasted at a cab-drivers' coffee-stall before he went back to his hotel, and she to her apartment in time to change into her office clothes.

    Meanwhile Iris herself had enjoyed a minor triumph. A recent poem of hers had been noticed by Edward Marsh and read at a meeting of the Georgian Poetry Society in London by none other than her sister Viola. Her own familiar words, recited in those other familiar tones, seemed to come winging back to her across the Atlantic:

> The days come up as beggars in the street
> With empty hands, as summer without sun
> That brings no gold of corn. With weary feet
> We tread our ways not caring where they run.
>
> The poet's song all golden in his throat
> Turns to a blood-red carpet, rage unfurled;
> The hunter's horn has made its little note
> A trumpet blast that shall awake the world.
>
> From silent shores where languid tides have swept,
> From quiet hills where dreaming people reign,
> Strange eyes drop water that have never wept
> Men rush to slaughter that have never slain.
>
> For look! the gorgeous armies marching onwards,
> And look! the draggled line, the feet that lag,
> The burning banner, and returning homewards
> The pallid faces and the bleeding flag!
>
> From house to house the mournful winds have blown
> The dying war-cry in the watchers' ears,
> From heath to hill have borne the weepers' moan
> Have drowned the drum, have frozen up their tears.
>
> They see the dusty roads of separation
> They see the lonely seas and strange lands.
> Their children give good bodies for the nation
> And yield their swords to death with loyal hands.

5) Curtis Moffat

6a) Viola and Iris in fancy dress

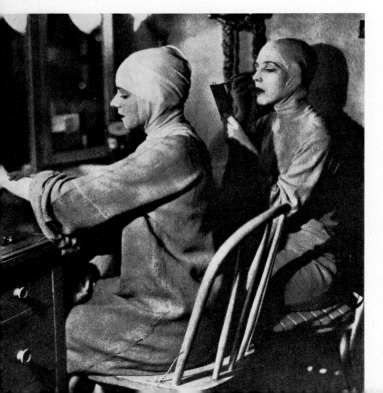

6b) Iris and Diana Manners making up for 'The Miracle'

Beggar and Prince in meeting face to face
Hold the same secret shining in their eyes –
The awful terror of a fierce disgrace,
The awful hope that glory may arise,

The hope that like a flame from the black field
Flings up its prophecy on fervent wings;
Pride in the strength of God whose sword we wield,
And charity the only crown of kings.

For his birthday that year Iris presented her father with a silver egg-cup engraved with the words 'For the Beloved Egg-otist'. He accepted such teasing from her, recognizing it as the manifestation of a high-spirited nature which he had never been able to control as fully as in his two other daughters. With Viola, for instance, he had always exercised complete authority through mutual love and understanding. When he commanded she obeyed instinctively. She was little more than a baby, splashing in the sea with him, when he removed his enfolding arms and said, 'Float!' and she had floated like a cork. She had just begun to ride and was still on a leading-rein when he released her, saying, 'Come and ride with me, dear,' and she had cantered after him on her pony. In the role of Ariel she had stood dithering with fright in the flies, harnessed to the wire which would pull her through the air, when his voice commanded from below, 'Fly!' and she had immediately launched herself into space. 'Now sing!' he then cried, and quaveringly she had broken into '*Where the bee sucks there suck I*'.

But with Iris the most he could do was warn her against too much levity – 'laughter can be killing' he told her – and put her on her guard against figures he considered too notorious, including even some of his own Bohemian friends, such as Isadora Duncan. He need not have worried unduly. His daughter's life was anything but 'fast', and, as she herself wrote to Sybil:

> My passion for the male sex is entirely unsatisfied. I dream morbidly of horrible meetings with rakish cinema stars, and

amours with a half broken buffoon. All are immune to the beauty of circles and the intoxication of the jolly-laide. To comfort myself in failure I plunge into readings of Gorki, Archibetzoff and the like, sinking with a sigh of contented cynicism and the word 'dust' on my lips.

Shortly afterwards, however, she met a young painter, Curtis Moffat, at a party in New York. His looks and manner attracted her at once. He spoke softly and slowly, and an air of indolence added to his charm. His eyes contained a quizzical expression and his smile was sometimes melancholy. His forehead was that of an intellectual, his fine dark brown hair already beginning to recede.

His family had once been rich and owned a house in Dinard where he had spent most of his childhood, but their fortunes had now dwindled and he was struggling to make a living. Nevertheless his tastes were sybaritic; he enjoyed good food and wine, and collected *objets d'art*.

To Iris there was something mysterious and occult about his presence; he looked like a prentice wizard or magus out of a fairy story, especially in the black cloak he habitually wore at night when he took her out to explore the more raffish quarters of the city: the Bowery, Harlem, Greenwich Village and the dockside. When Sir Herbert heard about these expeditions he was horrified, especially as he was due to go on tour again and Iris insisted on staying behind. There was a good reason for her insistence, as she explained to Sybil:

> I have been staying with Mrs Sawyer by the sea where was my young love Moffat with whom I spent the entire days and nights. You would, I think, like him very much as he is worth the praise.

When she told her father on his return that she wanted to marry Curtis, he refused even to consider the matter: 'Quite ridiculous, my dear, he may be a charming and unusual young man but he's much too poor and you're both too young.' But once again, in December 1916, he had to leave on tour and Iris remained in New York where a few days later she and Curtis were invited to a party where the Mayor happened to be present. Hearing that he had the right to perform marriage services, they persuaded him to marry them there and then, with a couple of other guests acting as their witnesses.

Sir Herbert was understandably hurt by what he considered a feckless disregard for his feelings, and shocked by what he regarded as a travesty of a wedding. He insisted on a second, more orthodox ceremony being carried out and meanwhile cabled an announcement of his daughter's engagement to the English Press. 'Of course, if it pleases you,' Iris agreed, 'but I'll just be another whore bride!'

Her father's disapproval was soon dispelled by the qualities he recognized in his son-in-law: physical grace and sartorial elegance, a philosophical turn of mind, a felicitous manner of self-expression (he was an entertaining talker, a good correspondent, and his handwriting was remarkably beautiful), quick wits and powers of concentration (he was an excellent chess player and had even invented a two-dimensional chess board for his own use and amusement). He admired him, too, for taking fencing lessons, and understood his passion for betting on horses. It was with genuine affection, therefore, that he presented him as a wedding present with a slim gold watch engraved with the words:

> May this watch keep time
> And time keep you.

Thus Iris followed the example of her two sisters in marrying despite the initial disapproval of her parents. (Just before the war, Felicity, like Viola, had become secretly engaged to her future husband, Geoffrey Cory-Wright, while he was still at Cambridge, and had been given permission to marry only after he came back from France on a month's leave after being wounded in action.) But Sir Herbert made a flying visit to England and managed to convince Maud that Iris had made a perfect match. He also went to see the spectacular musical play *Chu Chin Chow*, which he had allowed his friend Oscar Asche to present at His Majesty's. Although he did not think the style of 'this oriental pantomime' was worthy of his beautiful theatre, and described it as being 'more navel than millinery', he invested £2,000 in it and Iris was allotted some of these valuable shares.

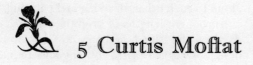 5 Curtis Moffat

When Sir Herbert got back to New York, Iris and Curtis were still on their honeymon in Nassau. In place of a wedding ring she wore round the third finger of her left hand a slender chain – a symbol of servitude which paradoxically betokened her freedom. Exulting in her happiness, she wrote to Sybil Hart-Davis:

> You do not know, nor can I fully realize, the relief at no longer questioning of each dull or hectic day, where it may finish, how dwindle, how exceed. . . . To be loved entirely without doubt, without harness, without limit, endlessly, overpoweringly and to be free, sole heir to the beauty of the whole earth, no mate tied to a desk or pinioned to a typewriter, and though penniless, willing to scour the entire world for delight and loveliness – Spain, London, Russia, China, why not? Oh, and in many disguises and phases: an artist's palette and a poet's pen – very idyllic!

They lived in a bungalow rented from the Colonial Hotel and were looked after by a black houseboy who was a thief but delighted them by reciting Byron as he cooked and served at table. They spent their days swimming, beach-combing for shells and sea-jewels of glass worn smooth and frosted by salt water,

The Rainbow Picnic

riding along the coral sands and into the turquoise sea, reading aloud to each other, drawing and painting.

    Iris bought lengths of brightly coloured cloth woven and hand-dyed on the island, and ran up Gauguin-like dresses of her own design. Drugged with content she found it almost impossible to write letters. Her output of poetry increased, however, and she had a small book of verse printed locally which included this poem dedicated to Curtis:

> Many things I'd find to charm you,
> Books and scarves and silken socks,
> All the seven rainbow colours
> Black and white with 'broidered clocks.
> Then a stick of polished whalebone
> And a coat of tawny fur,
> And a row of gleaming bottles
> Filled with rose-water and myrrh.
> Rarest brandy of the 'fifties,
> Old liqueurs in leather kegs,
> Golden Sauterne, copper sherry
> And a nest of plovers' eggs.
> Toys of tortoiseshell and jasper,
> Little boxes cut in jade;
> Handkerchiefs of finest cambric,
> Damask cloth and dim brocade.
> Six musicians of the Magyar,
> Madness making harmony;
> And a bed austere and narrow
> With a quilt from Barbary.
> You shall have a bath of amber,
> A Venetian looking-glass,
> And a crimson-chested parrot
> On a lawn of terraced grass.
> Then a small Tanagra statue
> Found anew in ruins old,
> Or an azure plate from Persia,
> Or my hair in plaits of gold;
> Or my scalp that like an Indian

You shall carry for a purse,
Or my spilt blood in a goblet. . . .
Or a volume of my verse.

Her thoughts often turned to her father. 'My only anxiety and sorrow is not to see Daddy,' she wrote to Constance Collier. 'He was divine to us and I do love and admire him more than ever before. Do write and tell me about him. I should so hate him to think I were just enjoying myself and not caring about seeing him.'

By this time Iris was pregnant and, after so much tropical luxuriance, found herself longing for a less cloying, urban atmosphere. She and Curtis therefore set sail for Havana, but no sooner had they arrived than he fell ill and had to go into a nursing home. She stayed with him all day and every night, talking and reading aloud. While he slept she sat in the half-light of his room, returning in reverie to the buttercup fields of her childhood, hoping those happy memories would embrace the baby she was carrying.

> I am afraid my child will be a girl – and I like men so – I *like* them so! [she wrote to Sybil]. . . . You would be very happy here, and we could take great pleasure over simple things like tea with plenty of jam and bathing and reading and buying sweetmeats and faldorals and going out in a boat and betting on race-horses. We also could smoke together, which in itself is a pleasure, and the crabs here are huge and made of bright-red china. I wish you were here – I *wish* you were here.

The child – a boy – was born in February 1918, and christened Ivan.

Almost a year earlier, in April 1917, Viola also had given birth to a child; but hers was a girl. Since this was the very month America had entered the war, Sir Herbert characteristically cabled to his daughter: 'Best love, darling. Call her Virginia or Columbia.'

Meanwhile he was as tireless as ever in spreading propaganda in favour of the Allies. His patriotic feelings verged on jingoism and he was shocked by the pacifist views which Iris held, and indeed voiced: 'Mars will find me a rebel to the end and I would cut Napoleon if I saw him.' He even went so far as to modify the dialogue of a play if by doing so he could stir his audience appropriately. On the first night of *The Newcombs*, for instance, he inserted a toast to the British Navy which was greeted with cheers and applause, and ended one speech with the words, 'Colonel Newcombe begs respectfully to salute the star-spangled banner'. Sometimes, at the end of a performance, he managed to have them all on their feet singing in turn the anthems of England, France, Belgium, Russia and America. His efforts were duly recognized by Asquith, Balfour and Lloyd George, and when, later in the year, he came back to England via Spain, it was arranged for him to travel as King's Messenger from Madrid – a privileged position which, much to his delight, entitled him, a civilian, to cross from Calais to Dover with the troops.

He was overjoyed to be back in London and to see all his friends again. Invitations were showered on him and he accepted them all with avidity. For three weeks he led an intensely active social life, infecting all around him with his high spirits. Then, while staying away for the weekend, he had a bad fall downstairs and ruptured a tendon above the knee-cap. Back in London he consulted the eminent surgeon, Sir Alfred Fripp, who advised an immediate operation, and so he moved into Sir Alfred's own nursing home, Netley House, the very next day.

In the operating theatre he took the greatest interest in the preparations and, on his insistence, was at first given a mixture of gas and oxygen so that he might watch all the preliminaries for as long as possible before losing consciousness. When he finally went under, he murmured, 'Nirvana,' and then, 'I shall see you again.'

The operation was entirely successful and he was soon sitting up in bed holding court, surrounded by visitors. Maud brought him the manuscript of Flecker's *Hassan* to read, which he enjoyed so much that he planned to put it on at His Majesty's as soon as the run of *Chu Chin Chow* came to an end, and thereby exorcise his beloved theatre with a production of his own. A few days later, on 2 July, while his nurse was peeling a peach for him, he asked her to open the window. She did so and, on turning, saw his head fall forward. By the time she was by his side he was dead.

His death was subsequently attributed to the formation of blood clots. His brother Max, on seeing him next day, found his face

> both familiar and strange. Death, that preserves only what is essential, had taken away whatever it is that is peculiar to the face of an actor. Extreme strength of character and purpose was all that remained and outstood now. But at the corner of the lips there was the hint of an almost whimsical, an entirely happy smile. And I felt that Herbert, though he was no longer breathing, was somehow still 'radiant'.*

Herbert's heart had remained romantic until it ceased to beat. Back in Boston, Solita Solano received a letter from him postmarked 6 P.M. on the day of his death, asking her to come and work as a dramatic critic in London, and offering to use his influence with newspapers on her behalf.

His wife was stunned, stricken by the shock. His daughters grieved not only for the loss of a father but also of an adored companion and fellow-adventurer. Iris dedicated a poem to him:

> I cannot think that you have gone away.
> You loved the earth – and life lit up your eyes
> And flickered in your smile that would surmise
> Death as a song, a poem or a play.
> You were reborn afresh with every day,
> And baffled fortune in some new disguise.
> Ah! Can it perish when the body dies
> Such youth, such love, such passion to be gay?
> We shall not see you come to us and leave
> A conqueror – nor catch on fairy wing

* Max Beerbohm, *op. cit.*

The Rainbow Picnic

Some slender fancy — nor new wonders weave
Upon the loom of your imagining.
The world is wearier, grown dark to grieve
Her child that was a pilgrim and a king.

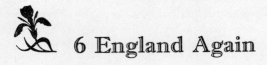# 6 England Again

As soon as Iris was able to travel she and Curtis returned to England with the infant Ivan, a black mammy and a bloodhound; and while Lady Tree was arranging a flat in Davies Street for them, they went to stay with Richard and Sybil Hart-Davis in Kent.

The two Hart-Davis children, Rupert and Deirdre, took to Iris at once, doubtless recognizing her own childlike quality and seeing in her a fellow-adventurer and rebel. 'I hope you are bringing up Rupert as an anarchist,' she had already written to Sybil from America. 'Begin now to show him the red shirt idea; fill him with desires to become the great anti-capitalist and so forth – seriously I think it is the only thing worth doing in these times. If I were not so lazy I should quickly become a bomb-thrower.'

Now she was able in person to encourage his sense of adventure. When he wanted to go for a ride in a cart drawn by a goat, despite his mother's objections to the 'very rough-looking man' in charge, she automatically sided with him. He was pleased, too, that she never tried to hoodwink him. On one occasion, for instance, when she and his mother were talking in French to prevent him from understanding the conversation, she noticed his perplexed curiosity and at once confessed: 'Yes, Rupert, we're talking about you!' Furthermore, she paid him the compliment of treating him like an adult and assuming his sense of humour was as highly developed and sophisticated as her own. A letter she wrote to him shortly after moving to London was typical of her attitude towards him.

> There is no news, except that the Albert Memorial fell on my left foot and completely spoilt my shoe, also I wear a live monkey in my hat and a frog in my button-hole.
> Buckingham Palace burnt yesterday which makes London nice and warm. I live in a small boat on the famous river Thames and eat fried shrimps for breakfast. Your mother rows the boat and I fry the shrimps' tails. We throw the scraps to any passing whale.
> This morning I fell into a pillar-box and was posted; I hate being posted.
>
> > Much love, dear Rupert,
> > from Iris.

To Deirdre, too, Iris was a 'magical golden figure'. The little girl used to share an enormous bed with her mother, and sometimes with her mother's female guests as well. For if Sybil turned up late at night from London bringing an unexpected woman friend, there was nowhere else to sleep – impossible, in those days, to make up another bed after the staff had retired, as linen cupboards were locked and the key kept by the housekeeper; sheets had to be aired and rooms prepared in advance. And so, on waking, Deirdre would peep across her mother to see if there was anyone on the other side. To discover Iris lying there was always a delight.

Iris was extremely fond of Richard Hart-Davis. She thought him handsome though somewhat prosaic, mocked him for being a member of the Stock Exchange, and in his company could not resist behaving eccentrically in order to tease him. One day while strolling along the front at Brighton with him, she said, 'I feel like going into the sea', walked down the steps leading to the beach, advanced fully clothed into the water until she was neck-deep, then rejoined him on the promenade and insisted on his taking her, dripping, to tea at the Metropole Hotel.

Another time, while out shopping with him in the village, she saw a horse and cart standing outside the butcher's shop. Springing on to the box, she seized the reins and with a crack of the whip set off at a spanking gallop down the main street, standing erect like the Charioteer of Delphi.

Even without resorting to such behaviour she often bewildered him. At one time her only luggage was a large, rather crumpled paper bag. Realizing this caused him embarrassment, the next time she came to stay she carried a suitcase. Little did he know it was completely empty!

When she and Curtis eventually moved into the Davies Street flat, they had an unpleasant surprise. Maud had apparently lost her gift for decoration and, in an effort to make the place cheerful, had picked out all the mouldings, plasterwork and panelling with over-bright gold paint and filled the rooms with ornate gimcrack furniture. The general effect, Iris felt, was of 'gilded squalor'. To make matters worse, no sooner were they installed than Curtis, who had not completely recovered from his illness in Havana, had a relapse and was forced to spend several months in bed. This did not prevent him, however, from practising his swordsmanship with a fencing master and he would thrust and parry propped up on the pillows.

After Iris had nursed him back to health and they were able to go out again, their company was eagerly sought by Bohemian society. They were often seen dining at the Eiffel Tower and drinking at the Café Royal. They also entertained lavishly at home, where Curtis himself did the cooking, producing masterpieces worthy of a professional chef.

As a married woman, Iris felt much less shy in society – 'I only blush when I'm spoken to,' she told Sybil – and was now at the apogee of her white and gold beauty, to which Curtis's dark good looks and air of mystery provided a foil. Entering a room together, they might have been taken for symbolic figures of Night and Day; and their very presence automatically enlivened the atmosphere of any party.

Viola and Iris had missed each other during their long separation. Viola had been the earliest and strongest influence in her younger sister's life. Something of a witch, she had taught Iris how to put a curse on an enemy, how to address the moon and, although innocent herself until womanhood, had instructed her in the technicalities of sex and the mysteries of love, drawing her like a siren below the surface depths of feeling, leading her in enchanted twilight to the ocean bed of deeper emotions. The close affinity that had since existed between them now enabled Iris to realize at once that her eldest sister, for all her courage and humour, was beset with material cares and unfulfilled longings.

Though Viola had attained her heart's desire in marrying Alan Parsons, and the life they shared was true and staunch, Iris felt it could have done with a coat of paint and a yard or two of cheerful bunting. The joyous radiant creature that was her eldest sister seemed constricted and confined, an aerial messenger earth-bound by humdrum necessity, a thoroughbred racehorse put between the shafts. Alan suffered from recurring bouts of asthma. These might have been alleviated in a warmer climate, but his job in the Home Office kept him in England — no hardship to him, for he loved London and disliked leaving it. But Viola yearned for sprees in the country where, on the rare occasions these occurred, she could bathe in rivers and streams, emerge with her long limbs plastered in watercress and dance barefoot on the grass, while pining for Italy and foreign travel. Healthy and resilient herself, she was baffled by her husband's ailment. 'Tis not so sweet now as it was before,' she thought, recalling the days when she had played Viola in *Twelfth Night*. At one time Alan used to accompany her songs on the piano and they would sit side by side on the old oak chest he had used as a piano stool at Oxford, picking and choosing excerpts from *Rosenkavalier*, *Ariadne*, *The Girl of the Golden West* and many other operas which they both knew by heart. But now, tired from the office, he preferred to spend the evenings reading or making entries in his commonplace book, and she sang alone.

With two sons and a daughter to bring up, she had had to renounce the stage and entertaining, both of which she had enjoyed. Having first taken a big house which was a constant drain on Alan's salary and her own small income, they had moved from one smaller house to another and eventually into a one-room flat, leaving their children in the care of Lady Tree. But she was still able to rejoice over small things. Her heart lightened as she saw the first spring flowers in London parks, the season's new fruit and vegetables in greengrocers' windows – 'Raspberries! But I've only got threepence. Can I have three?'

For some time, to eke out their joint resources, she worked for a Sunday newspaper. Her personal column, *Can I Help You?*, was designed to provide answers to correspondents seeking advice or information. Even in this relatively dull employment she managed to display humour and high spirits, and such was the success of her column that it was considered worth parodying by no less a personage than Ada Leverson, 'The Sphinx', Oscar Wilde's most faithful friend.

Question

I would like to become a ——. Should I have to become a ——? I should prefer a monastery if possible out of England. I am an excellent climber. If I get on could I keep up my music and dancing?

Answer

Your letter is so illegible I cannot read if you wish to become a monk or a monkey. I will answer for both or either. The latter would be frightfully easy for you, keep up your climbing, nutcracking and chattering. Just be yourself and if you pass your exam you might get into the Zoo. I see no objection to your keeping up your music and dancing. On the other hand you wish to become a monk – but I can't read the word. What a bore you are.*

Her father's death had been a crushing blow to Viola, for she had always relied on him for guidance, encouragement and comfort. Gradually, however, another actor-manager, Gerald Du Maurier, came to take his place as counsellor and friend.

---

* Violet Wyndham, *The Sphinx and Her Circle*, a memoir of Ada Leverson by her daughter (André Deutsch, 1963).

Her semi-romantic relationship with him gave her a new lease of life and, as she confided to Iris, seemed to restore her youth with 'games and tricks of the palpitant heart'. In 1923 they collaborated on *The Dancers*, which he duly produced at Wyndham's Theatre and in which Tallulah Bankhead made her first London appearance. It was highly successful and throughout its run Viola, as part author, earned between £70 and £100 a week. As both she and Alan were prodigal by nature, they spent most of each weekly windfall on entertaining their friends. Meanwhile she had recovered all her gaiety and often indulged, like Iris, in spontaneous clowning. On the Du Mauriers' yacht in Fowey Harbour she (deliberately?) fell overboard. Heedless of the unsuitable clothes she was wearing – a long silk dress and a garden-party hat trimmed with a wreath of roses – she swam round and round the boat shouting: 'Lovely! Lovely!'

While Iris had been away in America, her schoolfriend Nancy Cunard had likewise published a volume of verse, *Sublunary*, which was praised by the Sitwells and reviewed enthusiastically by George Moore. She, too, had married. But her marriage had come to an end. She had resumed her maiden name and was now living by herself, having quarrelled with her mother. She and Iris became close companions again. Their friendship was spiced with a certain sense of rivalry, however, which was all the more acute since they tended to attract the same people. Iris was wounded when she realized that Sybil had, as she put it, 'rallied to Nancy's colours' during her absence:

> I was at first jealous, then pained, but in saner mood I realize that there was no cause for envy or distress. You never could love her more than me, though some dark intellectual woman (still beautiful at forty-five) might hold your affections from me for a time. You love Nancy as I do, because she is always unexpected the same as one expects, always the same and always surprising. One loves the fun with her and from her, and the ease of her company. One loves her squirrel movements and her squirrel's fur and eyes. Her abandon-

7a) Friedrich and Iris

7b) Friedrich and Boon

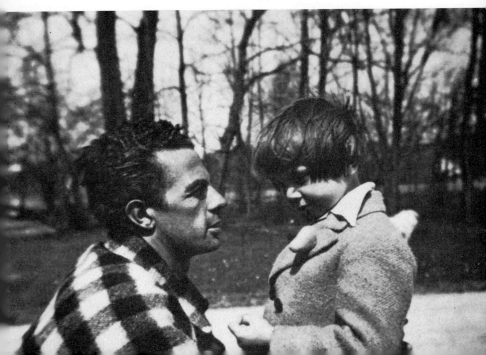

8) Iris in California

ment to pleasure, her priesthood to it. She skates and walks on stepping-stones, she is a djinn in a pocket-flask.

But I am solid, a quality perhaps overlooked in my general splendour. I am your sane love, critical of you; I take you at my own worth (not yours) which is limitless. Under all affectations, fringe, wantonness, decay, having cracked me you will find the kernel of the nut.

Curtis found Nancy the most interesting of Iris's friends. He shared her taste for the exotic and helped her to collect the ivory and wooden bracelets she subsequently always wore. His quiet, caressing voice soothed her aggressiveness and, in the course of an evening, often turned her anger into laughter.

Meanwhile Ivan had grown into an attractive, intelligent and amusing little boy but, to Iris's regret, 'he has not got one red hair on his head, which grieves me'. She enjoyed reading aloud to him and encouraged his talent for mimicry:

'Now do Daddy tasting wine, Ivan.'

'All right – if you do "Mameena" in her garden.' ('Mameena' was the grandchildren's nickname for Lady Tree.)

But though she loved her son and was proud of him, she had no deep maternal instincts – there was always a nurse to look after him, and afterwards, as he grew older, a governess – and when she wanted to escape from domesticity, she used to send him to stay with her mother, in company with his cousin Virginia.

'Mameena' adored and was adored by her grandchildren. Well might Lytton Strachey think her puns 'old cheese',* they revelled in them and roared with delight when there was haddock for breakfast and she lifted the cover of the dish and declaimed: 'Cry haddock and let slip the dogs of war!' Irresistible, too, was the way she inveighed against the cook who served too many casserole dishes, shaking her fist at the steaming pot and

* 'I suppose Lady Tree's style is "old cheese" to you, but I was completely bowled over by her punning humour and high spirits, no wonder Iris is such a steel to sharpen wits on. And again I am not surprised that she prefers Lady Tree's company to any husband.' Letter to Lytton Strachey in *Carrington's Letters and Extracts from her Diaries*, chosen by David Garnett (Jonathan Cape, 1970).

The Rainbow Picnic

declaring in an exaggeratedly histrionic tone: 'Curse – er – ole – cooking!'

By this time Iris and Curtis had moved out of Davies Street into a top-floor flat in Fitzroy Square. Unable to make a living from painting, Curtis had turned to decorating and their new home reflected his taste: dark walls relieved with chromium and mirror glass, rare and exotic woods, African masks and Benin heads. The kitchen was combined with the dining-room – a rare feature in those days – and round the corner, in Fitzroy Street, he had a shop where he sold rare objects and materials. He had also made a reputation as an avant-garde photographer, and was now in partnership with Olivia, Richard Wyndham's sister.

Dick Wyndham had all the qualities Iris most admired in a man: in her own words, 'rip, grip, smash and dash'. He was tall, handsome, athletic, fastidious, a good horseman, a connoisseur of fine wines. (The cellar he assembled in his Wiltshire house was a byword, and later he and Curtis became committee members of A. J. Symons's Wine and Food Society.) Iris not only shared these gastronomic pleasures but regarded them as symbols of *volupté*. 'Stay me with flagons, comfort me with apples, for I am sick of love' held an appeal for material solace which she could well understand; had she not written to Sybil in the dawning of their friendship: 'Promise to love me more than sugar cakes and jam'?

By 1924 Iris and Curtis had begun to be more independent of each other. She still wore the symbolic chain on her wedding-ring finger but her heart was not confined to him alone – nor did he expect it to be – and though they lived under the same roof in London, she was often on her own in Paris where she had acquired a small attic apartment on the Quai d'Orléans – 'not the hot Paris you know,' she wrote to Maud Nelkie (now Maud Russell), 'but a brown velvet Paris. It's such a good life – good to taste and good to look at, drink, think about and smell.'

Here she found Nancy Cunard again, involved in left-wing politics and Left Bank intellectualism, immersed in a love affair with Louis Aragon, and about to found The Hours Press which

England Again

subsequently printed a number of *avant-garde* volumes including a 'plaquette' of Iris's poems.

Another friend, who stayed with her at Quai d'Orléans, was the Polish painter Sophie Fedorovitch, whom she had first met in the Eiffel Tower Restaurant, in London, with Augustus John. 'She painted by day and made her living by night as a taxi driver. At midnight in her peaked cap and gauntlet gloves, this tiny, brave creature would dare the ruffian streets driving old roués to their assignations in Montmartre or through the Bois de Boulogne where "down and outs" would conk any head for a few francs.'*

In the midst of her Bohemian life, however, Iris's thoughts would revert to her mother, husband and son, and she wrote to Ivan:

> It is Easter time my darling. Oh! I hope it will be sunny on Easter Day and that Mameena will be there – if so you must pick some wild flowers for her – she likes them better than eggs. Darling, are you growing up strong and wise? You dress yourself now of course and I hope you are thinking of lots of things to tell me and talk about when I come back. For instance can you shoot well with your bow and arrow? Can you hit the target? The bull's-eye is pretty difficult but one can do it in the end.
>
> We will have a tournament when I come back.
>
> I hope you are practising jumping too – we will have a competition.
>
> And are you eating plenty, my dear lad?
>
> Much love, my only pink sparrow.
>
> > Your own,
> > Mother.

That year she spent part of the summer with Augustus and Dorelia John at Alderney Manor in Dorset. The sun blazed down

---

* From *Sophie Fedorovitch*, tributes and attributes printed for private circulation after her death in 1955.

Sophie Fedorovitch was a Russian artist who designed *décor* and costumes for many of the finest English ballets. She eventually became one of the artistic advisers to Sadler's Wells Ballet.

The Rainbow Picnic

from midsummer's day until harvest time, scorching the fields and baking the rounded hills like a batch of brown cottage loaves in the oven of the heat-wave. The house, which stood in the midst of wild heath lands, had a circular walled garden with a pond surrounded by cushions of pinks and pansies and a stockade of sunflowers and hollyhocks. Here, everyone gathered at teatime. Here too, since the nights were so stifling, a great communal bed of bracken was constructed, on which the entire household slept under the harvest moon, to be woken in the morning by the clamour of a bell summoning them to a breakfast of porridge and cream.

Every guest was allotted some kind of outside work. Iris was set to tarring a fence. A Polish friend who had come with her mended the wall. Francis Macnamara, Dylan Thomas's future father-in-law, minded the farm and also tutored the children. Dorelia's sister, Edie McNabe, milked the cow, made butter and bread, bottled fruit and collected wild honeycombs. The little girls, Vivien and Poppet, amused themselves and everyone else by riding the pigs, while their brother Romilly, aged fifteen, philosophized on the evils of lust and drink.

John himself sat silent and withdrawn, puffing his pipe and delighting in the sight of his wife and daughters in long faded cotton dresses and burnt straw hats, and Iris in a French fisherman's smock of blue coarse linen. At dusk, as the shadows lengthened, he would ruffle his shaggy mane and say, 'How about driving over to the *White Hart* or the *King's Arms?*' Whereupon ponies were caught and harnessed to traps, and the company clip-clopped off to one of the pubs where they played shove-halfpenny and drank pink gins.

In the autumn Iris wrote to Sybil urging her to be her companion on a roving journey to Germany: 'Do come, it would be an adventure at all events and I feel I ought to go even if only to put it out of my mind.' But Sybil was very ill and on the verge of a nervous breakdown. (She died early in 1927.) Iris then advised

long readings out loud of perhaps Dickens or Proust. Some slow quiet story unfolding itself chapter by chapter till one has no life of one's own. Mother read *Great Expectations* to me when I was in bed this summer and it was so *pleasant*. . . . I am disappointed about Germany but never really thought we should get off together, though I should have loved it with you. I will somehow manage it, as it is a pity to fail in one's ideas because of trains or rooms.

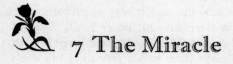 ## 7 The Miracle

Since Iris's return to Europe, her childhood friend Diana Manners had married Duff Cooper, Sybil's brother, and also made a name for herself as an actress, particularly in the part of the Madonna in Max Reinhardt's play *The Miracle*, which had had a very successful tour in America. In 1925 she rejoined the cast for the Salzburg Festival, to which she and Iris motored together. The play was scheduled for a second American tour later in the year and, since the actress playing the Nun would not be available then, Diana suggested that Iris should be engaged for the part.

In spite of her theatrical background and gift for mimicry, Iris was appalled by the very idea of performing in public, on a stage; but Diana eventually persuaded her to be 'tried out' by Reinhardt in the privacy of his castle nearby. The audition was postponed from day to day, and Iris grew more and more nervous. The weather, the landscape itself, the very elements seemed to conspire against her. The leaden sky weighed down upon her; the surrounding mountains confined her as though in a strait-jacket; the howling wind drowned the sound of her voice as she rehearsed her part alone in an attic.

When Reinhardt summoned her at last, all he asked of her was to read the Lord's Prayer out loud. No other test was required; the beauty of her voice, the grace of her movements, the whiteness of her skin convinced him at once; he engaged her as the Nun then and there.

Diana was delighted. She had dreaded the prospect of being separated so long from Duff, knowing all too well the torments of anxiety she suffered when she was away from him, plagued by thoughts of accidents or illnesses which might befall him during her absence. But with Iris at hand to bolster up her courage and laugh at her fears, she embarked for America in a very different frame of mind.

Throughout the tour she and Iris were looked after by Reinhardt's *homme de confiance*, Dr Rudolf Kommer, an enchanting little man with a spherical silhouette, a face as pale and full as a hay-harvest moon, a dimpled chin, a blob of a nose, and dark velvety eyes. Diana he already knew and worshipped: he called her the 'gentle gazelle' and described himself as 'prostrated on the knees of my heart' before her. Iris he at once envisaged as 'the derelict nymph', and this was the name by which she was henceforth known to him. To them he figured as 'Kaetchen', an endearing name which conjures up that of a German lady's maid, and indeed he was their faithful, lovelorn, sorely-tried servitor and duenna.

He it was who acted as their go-between with Reinhardt, who smoothed their way across America, who booked their hotel suites for them, who even tucked them up in bed (as a special treat for him, so they said), who took charge of their money (Iris was apt to stuff her weekly pay-packet into a pocket of her grey military great-coat, bequeathed to her by an officer friend in the Brigade of Guards, from which it invariably disappeared) and who offered himself as a willing butt for their practical jokes and teasing.

Together they bought a monkey (another 'treat for Kaetchen', of course!) which behaved in characteristic monkey fashion, pulling faces at itself in the looking-glass, powdering its nose, eating grease-paint sticks, getting drunk and being sick in the middle of Diana's dressing-table. It was the despair of her English maid, Miss Wade. It was also an object of loathing to Kaetchen, especially when it seized his hat and brand-new umbrella, a present from Diana, and scampered off with them.

The Rainbow Picnic

He eventually got rid of the beast, but only after making a round of the zoos and pet shops until he found a dog mart willing to accept it.

Another, slightly more sour, apple of discord was young Raimund von Hofmannsthal, the son of the poet and dramatist Hugo von Hofmannsthal.

> Kaetchen had brought him to *The Miracle* as a means for him to work his passage to California, where he was to forge his fortune. He was nineteen, spoke no word of English, and the Kat could not miaow in French. He was Austrian, intelligent – and made in our mould, unlike the other supernumeraries. He was shy and strange and clearly needed protection and affection. . . . It was natural therefore that we should first invite him to drug-store snacks, and then to kitchenette meals in our flat. . . . Kaetchen disapproved of favouritizing one of a vast cast. He was jealous, so the drugstore snacks were criticized, and pot-luck at home could cause bad sulks. Raimund standing nightly at the stage-door as we came out and silently and very shyly offering me a cigarette would be enough to blanch Kaetchen like an almond. I fear that this attempted embargo upon him only sharpened our wish for Raimund's protection and company. He earned thirty dollars a week on tour, and had to travel (two men to a bed) on the special *Miracle* train. As we had promised Kaetchen not to pay for his snacks, the poor thing was reduced to quelling his hunger pains with the cheapest thing on the menu, a cheese sandwich at twenty-five cents. The growing boy often had to watch Iris savouring a juicy steak and me gobbling prawns and Russian dressing. In Kansas City, Kaetchen's supervision gone, he was with us at all times.*
>
> At one stage of the tour there was an interval of ten days without a performance. Diana and Iris decided to spend this time riding in Arizona and Mexico. Raimund was determined to go with them, and so telegraphed his father for some money to enable him to pay his own way. When Diana and Iris were apart from Kaetchen, they communicated with him daily,

* Diana Cooper, *The Light of Common Day* (Hart-Davis, 1959).

The Miracle

usually in doggerel verse which could be sung to such tunes as *There is a Tavern in the Town* or *One of the Rakish Kind*. The news of the trek in Mexico was therefore broken to him in the following cable:

> For fear of hold-ups on the road and birds of prey
> Two dolls who are so grave and gay
> Took a cavalier
> Not unrelated to a foreign bard
> But if our cat is black, why then
> All pleasure is marred.

On their return they were met by 'a jet black Kat', as opposed to the sleek white angora he was when in a good mood. (Rex Whistler indeed did a reversible drawing of him for Diana, one side depicting him as a purring white puss and the other as a witch's hell-cat.)

'Diana is a doll of purest china with a gold heart,' Iris told him, 'and I am a wooden doll with a heart of red flannel.' From then on they took to calling each other 'doll' and actually had two rag-dolls made to resemble themselves. Wade dressed these in clothes appropriate to their respective styles; Diana's mother, who had come from England to see *The Miracle*, painted their featureless faces realistically, and they were then given the names 'Dianetta and Risette'.

Shortly afterwards, when Diana and Iris were again temporarily parted from Kaetchen, they sent him a telegram announcing their return and asking him to meet them at the station. There he was on the platform when the train pulled in. But there was no sign of them. He checked the berths they were supposed to have booked against the numbers they had quoted in their telegram. They were unoccupied. He enquired of the sleeping-car attendant – who promptly produced, not Diana and Iris, but Dianetta and Risette.

Diana often felt homesick and expressed her yearning for England in her letters to Duff. Iris, characteristically, wrote to Ivan:

In Cincinnati
Everyone asked us to a party,

The Rainbow Picnic

Because we act in the Miracle,
And Americans are so hysterical;
But I like pirates better than people in towns,
And would rather have tea with you and some gipsies and clowns,
In the green woods amongst trees and creepers,
Providing there were no gamekeepers.
In Boston I lost and found all my week's profit.
Here is a dollar of it.
I wonder what you and Con and Mameena
Are having for deena. . . .
I eat octopus and buffalo and hyena,
Cooked by Red Indians in a circus arena.
I lasso my lunch, and fish for my breakfast,
Eat a whole whale, but always have an egg first.
I brush my hair with a live porcupine,
I wash my clothes in phosphorous brine,
And pin them with a cactus spine.
Rattlesnakes' skins and eagles' feathers
Keep one well dressed in all weathers.
My waggon is harnessed to a dragon.
I have a bicycle, made of a silver icicle
And no man but a snow-man do I see.
He sweeps the floor
And guards the door for me.
I live on a frozen lake,
In a frozen house like a wedding cake.
Then seven bears came to sup,
Each had his plate and cup,
But nothing to eat for tea,
Nothing to eat but me.
The bears are gone, the ice is gory,
That is the end of my story.

In the summer she made a flying visit to England and returned with Ivan and his governess. During the crossing she wrote to her mother:

> It was sad leaving you, so many of us going out of your sweetness over the sea – but thinking of you lovingly. . . . I

wonder have you set a pied à terre in the flat? I hope you will like it, you may if you tear the carpets from the floor and put your own bowls of roses and table cloths and daintiness everywhere. . . . 'Oh never cross to Dover said the pig in clover.'

Ivan was delighted this morning by seeing flying-fish and a red octopus. We sit and read in the sun, run races on the deck, there is a gymnasium and a swimming pool made of a tarpaulin umbrella turned upside down. We have good cabins and are happy and good. Food not so good – served in the spices of the menu-maker's imagination. He calls fried plaice 'Young Fair Isle Sole Himalaya' or roast mutton 'best leg of adolescent Salisbury lamb Henry IV'; the next day the same pale haunch is 'rose-fed new-laid Kentish lamb Gregorian' and so on, which is such a disappointment to the fly in the ointment!

Three days before the last performance of *The Miracle*, she and Diana went to a party given by Elinor Glyn, who was surrounded as usual by a large number of handsome men. To Iris, however, only one stood out, literally head and shoulders above the others: a giant in stature, with a lean, muscular body, thick, curly brown hair, dark-blue eyes, high cheek-bones, a deep melodious voice, a weather-beaten complexion: Friedrich Ledebur, scion of a noble but impoverished Austrian family.

After the party she told Diana that she had fallen in love and was going to stay on in America.

8 Friedrich Ledebur

Diana was shocked by Iris's abrupt and unexpected defection. She felt 'deserted for a whim, lonely and deceived in my affection',* and sailed for England, exhausted by the arduous tour and dispirited at the loss of her companion.

Kaetchen was likewise shocked by Iris's apparent determination to sacrifice everything and everybody for what he too regarded as a whim. He could hardly forgive her for abandoning Diana. His sentimental Austrian heart also bled for her husband, left high and dry in London, and her son, the boy with the 'Mozartian voice', fatherless in New York. But since he too had to stay behind in America in connection with Reinhardt's affairs, he felt responsible for her and never failed to answer any of her appeals for assistance or advice. In due course he even relented towards Ledebur and affectionately nicknamed him 'Uhlan', the name by which Iris addressed him for ever more, she in return being known to him as 'Bird'.

Curtis himself was badly shaken by the decisive rupture. He was accustomed to Iris's need for romantic interludes, but had never expected her to embark on a new, completely separate life with someone else. He wrote, more in despair than with conviction, asking her to come back, telling her he was redecorating her bedroom at Fitzroy Square in pale yellow, her favourite

* Diana Cooper, *op. cit.*

colour. But she was as deaf to his pleas as she had been to Kaetchen's admonitions. She continued to feel the deepest affection for him, but was incapable of pretence and compromise.

Meanwhile, life with Friedrich was not all plain sailing. His ambition was to be an actor, and his striking looks gave him every reason to hope for success on the stage or screen. But so far no opportunity had occurred and he therefore relied on his prowess as a horseman to provide him with a living. His services for breaking and handling horses were increasingly in demand and he would be summoned at a moment's notice to some distant ranch or stable. Iris never knew from one day to another when he was going away or how long he would be absent. Sometimes he would leave without even telling her his destination, and in desperation she would cable to Kaetchen: 'Send me Friedrich' or 'Where is Uhlan?'

To make matters worse, she was in more or less permanent financial straits. Time and time again, and always with the utmost tact and discretion, Kaetchen came to her rescue. Two hundred dollars would arrive on her birthday, a similar sum at Christmas, and one summer he invited her to sail to Europe with him for a 'continental tour. . . . Dearest, dearest derelict, do come. I undertake to bring you back to these United States early in the autumn.'

'My heart wears out my cloth,' she replied by cable. 'No shoes, no hat, coming naked but unashamed.'

Later on, to ensure that she had a certain sum of money on which to draw, he arranged with Brentano's to publish a volume of her poems. Exasperated by her unpunctuality in delivering the manuscript, he cabled: 'If you don't send your libertine verses in time I shall reduce your mulishly obstinate body to smashed potatoes. Feel wave of hate already rising although I am still your Kaetchen.'

When the book, *The Traveller*, eventually came out, he bought up the entire edition.

Shortly afterwards Iris discovered she was pregnant and, as usual, sought Kaetchen's advice. He was appalled and did his utmost to convince her that while still married to Curtis she could not be allowed to bear another man's child. Reluctantly she agreed to have an abortion. He made the necessary arrangements and booked her into a clinic for the operation; but at the last moment she changed her mind and decided to keep the child.

All he could hope for now was to keep her condition secret for as long as possible, and so he persuaded her to lie low somewhere unbeknown to her friends and family. She therefore headed for Provence to bide her time in the romantic little mediaeval village of Les Baux. Here, in due course, Friedrich joined her.

But not for long. There was no livelihood for him in Europe; he had to return to America. Without him Iris felt bereft. Not knowing where to turn for solace or advice, she decided to go to England, face Curtis and come clean to Diana, on whose goodness and compassion she knew she could rely. And indeed Diana straight away suggested a solution. For many years she had longed to have a child of her own and had even made a pilgrimage to Lourdes to pray for one. She volunteered now to adopt Iris's as soon as it was born, and worked out a plan for this to be done as discreetly as possible. It was decided that the child should be discovered in traditional foundling style, laid in a basket on the doorstep of the Coopers' house in Gower Street. Thus it need never be traced back to Iris, who in the meantime would continue to keep in hiding from her family and other friends.

But, as the time approached, Iris again changed her mind since she could not bring herself to be parted from the child. Diana was naturally disappointed, but soon after, to her infinite joy, she found that she too was with child – almost as though her condition was somehow dictated by Iris's, the seed germinating sympathetically, as it is said to do between female animals in close proximity.

And so Iris's child, a boy, was born on 15 February 1928 at the Farringdon Hotel, Gower Street – an address chosen at the time of the foundling plan on account of its nearness to the Coopers' doorstep. Her mother and sisters had been notified some time before and were therefore not taken by surprise. In fact a family discussion had already taken place over the choice of a suitable name. 'If it's a boy he ought to be called Christian,' Felicity had said. 'Iris has always been a pilgrim.' But to Iris herself he became known as 'Boon', since he was a boon and a blessing.

By this time Ivan and his governess had come back to England and were staying with Lady Tree in a big house at Enfield. When he was told that he now had a younger brother he sat down to write him a letter of welcome, using one of his father's quill pens. And in due course he met the baby, when his mother brought him to stay.

The nurse Iris had engaged was deeply impressed by her. 'I well remember the first glimpse I had of her,' she subsequently wrote.*

> She wore a red skirt, pale green (pea-green) jumper and her hair was worn in what we called a long bob, nearly to the shoulders. The style suited her but her mode of dress seemed very strange for those days, but there was always just that bit of something different about her which stood out.
>
> She was always hard-up. It was quite a common occurrence to hear her voice from the garden float through the nursery window at the top of the house: 'Nurse – lend me a shilling for cigarettes.' I can't remember getting those shillings back but no doubt some of them did turn up in due course.
>
> I hope Boon has not lost his wonderful smile. People often stopped to look at him and remarked on his happy expression. . . .

When he was three months old the baby was christened Christian Dion, his godparents being Diana and Kaetchen, but he continued to be called Boon. As she came out of the church, Iris gave the first person she met a silver coin – an old north-country custom – and the stranger in return wished the baby long life, good luck and happiness.

Iris obtained a divorce from Curtis at Reno in 1933 and next year married Ledebur, who had previously 'adopted' the

---

* In a letter to the author.

child so as to give him his rightful name. Boon showed promise of being as tall as his father, and had inherited the Beerbohm red-gold hair. When Ivan was told of the adoption he asked, 'Then will Boon now grow brown curls like Friedrich's?'

The Ledeburs' early married life in California was a nomadic adventure, a raggle-taggle gipsy existence, with times when there was precious little in hand to put to mouth.

'We live all the time in the caravan, sponging for baths here and there,' Iris wrote to Viola, 'mostly sleeping outside in a bag and under the redwood trees which are five thousand years old and as high as Saint Paul's.'

She had devised a system for taking a bath and simultaneously washing her clothes: she got into the tub wearing everything that needed laundering, soaped and rinsed the garments on her body, then removed them and hung them up to dry while she soaked naked in fresh water.

Ivan had remained in England to be educated, living mostly with his grandmother or Viola, but often seeing his father, whom he found fascinating though aloof, isolated in his own world and therefore a trifle intimidating.

Meanwhile Boon shared his parents' roving life.

Part Two

9 Austria and Ireland

It was in the early 1930s that I first met Iris and Friedrich, at Kammer, Elenore Mendelssohn's fairy-story castle in Upper Austria. I had bicycled out there with my first husband, Henry,* to stay with Raimund von Hofmannsthal and his wife Alice who were living in another part of the vast lakeside edifice.

Alice, *née* Astor, a friend and contemporary of mine, had a Red-Indianlike beauty: ivory-coloured skin, dark sultry eyes, shining black-brown hair parted in the middle and brushed smoothly back in a chignon pinned at the nape of an exceptionally slender neck.

The first thing that struck me about Iris was that famous swinging gait of hers:

> With what a waving air she goes
> Along the corridor! How like a fawn!
> Yet statelier.

Like Friedrich, she dressed in Austrian costume and dirndls suited her marvellously well. Sometimes she wore stalking clothes: short jackets made of grey *loden* with dark-green facings and buttons of stag's horn. Her skirt swirled as she walked and her legs were strong and shapely.

---

* Then viscount Weymouth, now the marquess of Bath.

The Rainbow Picnic

As for Friedrich's appearance, I was completely bowled over. Never had I seen a figure so handsome and distinctive. His riding boots were lovingly burnished by himself and gleamed like polished jet on his long horsemen's legs. At night he wore an embroidered silk or brocade waistcoat, or a short Austrian jacket, a white shirt, a Byronic cravat and a belt of fine silver chains linked with oval-shaped filigree medallions.

There was a strange atmosphere at Kammer, induced or at least exaggerated by the *Föhn*, the prevailing wind which seemed charged with a weird inexplicable melancholy, a nameless nostalgic distress. Nerves were laid bare, sentiments were unduly ruffled and, at the slightest provocation, tears would flow.

At full moon elaborate picnics were staged on a huge raft moored like an island in the middle of the lake and approached by a launch. Here we would find candle-lit tables laid for supper and a string quartet playing water-music, while we sat on till all hours of the night drinking *Bowle*, that delicious local mixture of hock and peaches tight-laced with brandy. At one of these parties, perhaps under the combined effect of *Bowle* and *Föhn*, Iris slipped quietly overboard and swam ashore. When the rest of us eventually landed we found her sitting at the water's edge, a vexed Rhine Maiden, indignant that none of us had heeded her disappearance.

Friedrich had a string of horses stabled at Kammer and I rode with him and Raimund every day. I enjoyed riding infinitely more than bicycling and was loth to leave the enchanted castle, but Henry was keen to pedal on. 'Cycling will make your legs grow fat . . . not so good for a boot then,' were Friedrich's last words to me.

Kammer was the nearest approach to a permanent home that Iris and Friedrich had so far known; but even here they seemed unable to settle down together for any length of time. One of them would leave while the other stayed behind, or else they would both leave and, depending on circumstances, go their separate ways before joining each other again. Thus in 1933 Iris wrote to Viola:

Friedrich is going to England to stay with the Hofmannsthals in May and I shall be uneasy, as you are about Gerald* at times. No, I shall not like that at all. I like him best in America where I knew him first. Here it's his own country and that's strange after always moving over huge dusty plains in funny clothes. . . . It is odd for him being back in a mediaeval country castle life with all its beliefs and disdains. In England he would be too big for cottages, too clean for Eiffel Towers,† too much with me for huntin', fishin' and shootin', too vague and restless for drawing games, so he'll have to be kept moving in country lanes and Bond Street leather shops.

Men are cumbersome, one has always to treat them like an illness or a madness; think of Daddy, Duff, Gerald, how they have to be humoured: 'he doesn't like dogs, draughts, noises, apple-pie, music'. Men never fuss about their women. . . . Cumbersome. Well, it can't be helped; you and I will live together some day, unencumbered – cockling and musseling when the children are all married with professions.

Though Iris and Friedrich were so often parted, she never resigned herself to his absence and wrote to him nostalgically:

This afternoon the sun came out and I went to look at the lake where we bathe in summer. It was pale blue and very still; ice is trying to catch it. There is a heaviness around my heart but it has no name or reason, just that it walks by the low-tide shores and hears unanswered calling – a bird somewhere? A dog? Perhaps snow is pressing. Ships are in harbour, the fishermen set sail. Is it you I am wanting, or just some obscure exhaustion of the soul after one of her journeys into secret and far places? Soul, sleep on your wings. . . . I talk to my soul for better company.

Later that year Iris rented a small villa at Rottingdean and her niece Virginia came to stay with her while Viola was acting in a play. Together they went for long sea-walks and played

* Gerald Du Maurier.
† The Soho restaurant.

drawing games. When Viola's two sons joined them Iris told hair-raising ghost stories, frightening herself as well as the children with her inventions, and delighting them with her imaginativeness in games of 'Murder'.

But this domestic seaside interlude was of short duration. Soon afterwards she had re-embarked on her nomadic life. London she found 'ugly and barren. When Daddy and the theatre were gone,' she wrote to Viola, 'all the real flavour was lost. Glottenham I see as perpetual autumn, autumn at its best – hops and nuts, mud and blackberries. . . .'

For some time, lured by the siren songs of her friends Lillian Gish and Greta Garbo, she and Friedrich even went back to California; but the plays and scenarios by which she hoped to earn a living were never commissioned, nor were the film tests she was persuaded to take any more successful. Furthermore, as she again wrote to Viola, 'Friedrich seems now less excited about this country, lovely though it is . . . perhaps he would like Ireland, where he could hunt cheap. . . . I am terribly homesick for Ivan and Boon, otherwise well and happy.'

These were lean days for the Ledeburs, but once again Kaetchen turned up trumps, upbraiding Iris for what he called her 'financial feeble-mindedness' but simultaneously slipping her a cheque. When she and Friedrich eventually got back to England, Maud Russell proved herself a generous friend. 'I can now walk into Harrods with winged feet, much to the horror of the shoe department,' Iris wrote to her in gratitude for timely assistance.

Early in 1933 Alan Parsons died. From then on, Viola more or less abandoned the stage to concentrate on the upbringing of her children, for whom she found a perfect home: a vast rambling building which had once been a boys' school and now provided ample space for her own two boys and their sister Virginia to indulge in their hobbies and house their pets. The former dormitories and classrooms were converted into bedrooms and studios; the gymnasium became a playroom; bicycle polo was practised on the football field; the lockers contained secret treasures; the cloakrooms were glory-holes full of Wellington boots, fishing-rods and roller skates.

Austria and Ireland

Meanwhile Curtis still lived in London, playing an increasingly active part in the Wine and Food Society and confirming his reputation as an epicure. There was a memorable luncheon held at 4 Fitzroy Square in July 1936, 'when the host was Curtis Moffat supported by his son Ivan',* and the guests were Osbert Sitwell and André Simon.

The menu: Turbot en papillotes
              Pâtes au gratin
              Choux au lard
              Jambon
              Salade, fromage, fruits

The wines: Hugell's Riesling Réserve 1923
              Château de Cheval Blanc 1921
              Grande Fine Champagne Jubloteau 1906

'How Curtis manages to get hold of wines beyond the reach of all but millionaires is his secret but there is certainly no greater artist to show them off,' A. J. Symons subsequently reported.

Another meal was arranged on the spur of the moment by telephone, 'on the staff's night out', for the comparing of two bottles of Lafite '65. 'Smoked salmon proved a mistake; we were glad to clear our palates with baked potatoes slightly salted and peppered.'†

And on yet another occasion Curtis and his friends broached a bottle of some rare white Chartreuse: 'a curiosity Curtis had carried round with him for more than 10 years, with a penetrating, even stunning aniseed nose'.

Eventually he remarried, his second wife being Kathleen Allen. Small, very slim and brown-haired – a complete contrast to Iris – she preferred to dress in unobtrusive muted colours. Her taste in jewellery – small crosses and lockets, narrow rings of simple stones set in a circle – also underlined the contrast to Iris's chunks of amber, turquoise beads and heavy gold chains. Furthermore, she liked plain American Colonial furniture. She ate very little

---
* *Wine and Food Society Report.*
† *Ibid.*

The Rainbow Picnic

and preferred gin to wine, but even so regarded alcohol as a sustaining medicine to be taken only when necessary.

The difference between his two wives, in short, was akin to that between flaming sunset and pale moonlight, and from this he derived a certain comfort.

For some time after their return to England, Iris and Friedrich stayed with the von Hofmannsthals at Hanover Lodge, Regent's Park, in great luxury, and there were many 'wild nights with the cronies'. She and Viola went to the Chelsea Arts Ball together:

> I can remember staying up to watch them go off and they were dressed all ready for the ball in specially made dresses – Iris as the knave of hearts and my mother as the queen – but they were both so disappointed in the look of themselves that they slashed up some trousers of my father's and jackets of my brothers, got jam-jars for tiddlers, dirtied their faces and were ready to go.*

But London was no less 'ugly and barren' than before, and Iris's thoughts turned more and more towards the past. In letter after letter to Viola she nostalgically recalled the days of their youth:

> I remember a particularly rich period, about the first *Pinkie and the Fairies*, with parties at Walpole House, Alan and the Shakespeare Festivals, Pavlova but not yet Nijinsky, the Irish Players, Billy, Julian, Patrick, Edward H.†. . . . Everyone read Meredith at that time and was like his books.
>
> But I ramble on. It was leaving Walpole House that broke this period, all was quite different from then; you turned to Italy and, later, I to America – then the war. I never got completely back into England from America – His Majesty's had gone which was our root; the *jeunes filles* were all married or emancipated, the young intellectuals had crystallized into different groups. Ottoline Morrell was not there to keep a

---

* Letter to the author from the marchioness of Bath, *née* Virginia Parsons.

† Billy and Julian Grenfell, Patrick Shaw-Stewart, Edward Horner, all killed in the 1914–18 war.

flowing interchange, the illicit flaming orgies of George Moore*
and Cavendish were succeeded by sprightly every day binges
at the Holdens. Sybil was exiled at Bexley, Diana at low ebb
from leg-break and other people's disappointment in her
marriage and only the Tower† remained rebelliously carrying
on. The war atmosphere harboured the unsettled spirits, the
defeated Peter Pans, the moths (Nancy‡ especially).

It was not a good period, everyone was poorer and disillusioned after the blaze and havoc of war, with its loves
and deaths. Came sterility, pansies, Tallulah. For us no Glottenham or Brancaster, no Shakespeare, and the children were
in the bad stage of school, measles and brown coats, *and* I
suppose, no money.

I wonder what Daddy would have done? Would his genius
have survived the slump and change, found plays? Or would
he have gone touring as he meant to – to Australia and have
become uprooted?

I don't think the grand romantic would have prospered,
nor the classic, nor any revivals then.

Or again:

> I long for Mother and Daddy young again and everything
> fresh like daffodils.
> Life should be as a tree bearing fruit and dying, then burgeoning with leaves after winter – perhaps it is.

But when Viola received a spirit message from Sir Herbert, Iris
reassured her in an unusually down-to-earth manner:

> The message from Daddy is very strange and if true, even
> then unlikely – adding apprehension beforehand. But do not
> be troubled, if such things are really ordained then there *is*
> some plan to them and that is comforting; it is the thought
> of accident and stupidity, of the cruelty of nature and the
> indifference of the gods which is so terrible.

* George Gordon Moore, American millionaire.
† The Eiffel Tower Soho restaurant.
‡ Nancy Cunard.

The Rainbow Picnic

> It is lovely to think that spirits can talk with us but of course it's nearly always those doubtful, crankish, humourless people who become mediums, never you or Diana or even priests and Aunty Dora.*

As Iris had foreseen, Friedrich soon grew restless in London, and so they headed for Ireland, from where she wrote:

> This is a great change of scene after Hanover Lodge; complete isolation; no telephone for 2 miles; no shops for 8 miles; the stretch of a sandy bay before meadows and sandy hills behind. Inside the little house a deaf cook and 2 blue cats. But I like it all very much except for the cold. Fireplaces are the worst invention in the world of warmth; any old workman's bucket is more practical and if the room by dint of logs and coal gets warm at last the passage outside is like the deck of an icebound ship. However, all this is decadence – one is far too coddled.

Ireland suited them both. Friedrich was lent horses and so got all the hunting and racing he wanted; and Iris felt it provided an opportunity for Boon to lead the ideal life she had envisaged when, little more than a child herself, she had written to her school friend Maud:

> If by the grace of heaven I ever have children I shall send them for about a year at the age of 10 to some farm, alone with healthy brown peasants, where they can be in the mud and steal pears and get killed as much as they want to.

Now she wrote to Maud again:

> I am very happy here, completely cut off from any social excitements so that one forgets that language.
> I have a lovely house on an estuary with a large decayed park full of trees, green grass growing to the edge of a muddy watery stretch – beyond it hills flaming with gorse. Pony carts again, which I find delicious, high tea, picnics and Boon all to myself, no governess.

* Dora Beerbohm, who became a Sister of Mercy.

London is for Hutchinson,* Duff and Gracie Ansell.† But why Gracie? I can imagine her also in Florida getting florider and florider. London is for the Duchess‡ (Diana's), all the Stracheys and Curtis (since he has gone so native on it) and as for the English countryside, it is a shivery place most often.

There is a coldness, a reasonableness in London that affronts me, something in the look and noise of Regent Street, the gloom of Cadogan Road, the forlorn ugliness of Tottenham Court Road and the A.B.C. shops, the cockney beauty, the half cold, the damp, the soot. . . .

I tell you this country's greener than ever – wild and what I like. Strong and gorsey with sea and inlets; villages far apart and muddled together, tinkers, donkeys, charming ragged strangers, myths and fairies and ever-changing sky, suffusing soft lights.

But there is poverty – poverty with charm – meaning decayed estates, noble horses with broken harness and the indolence and grace which comes from patchedness and caring little, but there is also poverty of sunlight, of creation; no excess and overflow; no music and dancing, no glittering and carved churches; no fanciful attire; no butter, no oil nor garlic. . . .

The beauty is veiled in mist and mysticism; none of Mexico's gay hats and purple immensities. It is the country for the shy poet. I waver between the two and find my feet and the hot-water bottle.

Primitive conditions in beautiful surroundings appealed to Iris's romantic sense and also to her sense of humour. When two visitors from England, Joan Eyres-Monsell§ and Penelope Chetwode,¶ came to seek her advice on the riding tour they were planning and asked her whether they should take a pony and

* St John Hutchinson, barrister, known as 'Red Hutch', to distinguish him from 'Black Hutch', pianist and night-club entertainer.
† Notorious London personality between the wars.
‡ Violet Duchess of Rutland.
§ Now the Hon. Mrs Leigh Fermor.
¶ Now Lady Betjeman.

trap or a spare horse to carry baggage and fodder, they felt quelled when she replied: 'I would only take a saddle-bag slung on my horse, but then I am a super-woman.'

But life for the Ledeburs was not always pared down to bare essentials. They often stayed at Castle MacGarrett for shooting and race parties with Lord and Lady Oranmore and Browne. Their fellow-guests naturally included a good many hearties and Iris used to implore Oonagh Oranmore not to put her between a brace of these at dinner since she was either stricken dumb or would unconsciously begin to imitate them. She winced at the language some of them used and, like Oonagh, objected to their referring to the women who joined them at the shooting lunches as 'the bitch pack'. (One poor girl was so used to such terms that when walking through a boggy field behind one of the guns, on hearing him bellow, 'Sit, you bitch!', she obediently squatted in the mud, not realizing that the command had been given to an over-eager retriever!)

There was one sporting habitué of Castle MacGarrett, however, whom Iris found extremely attractive – Captain Eric Meiville, a Swiss international horseman who lived in Kildare where he had a stud. He was a friend of Friedrich's, who admired his expertise in the saddle. 'Friedrich, I believe you exchanged me with the Captain for a horse!' Iris used to say. A trim, well-turned-out figure, he had led an adventurous life and delighted Iris with his tales of derring-do. She used to watch him schooling his hunters and, in order to shine in his eyes, even nerved herself to take them over the jumps. He liked a woman to be elegantly clad, preferably wearing a feminine little black dress with a string of pearls and a hat for lunch in a restaurant, for instance. Iris's motley therefore embarrassed him no end whenever he took her out to Jammat's or the Shelbourne, but he went on taking her out just the same.

Another sportsman to whom Iris was attracted was Bose Daly, the Master of the Kildare Hunt, so much so that at the hunt ball she declared her admiration and praised his 'knightly beauty'. He was highly embarrassed. She, next morning, remembering how she had 'laid it on with a trowel', was deeply ashamed. And his wife Diana, affecting indignation, remarked:

Austria and Ireland

'I can't make up my mind whether Iris is wildly attractive or utterly repulsive. . . . I rather think the latter.'

Friedrich enjoyed Ireland as much as Iris knew he would; but, as in the early days of their marriage, he frequently had to leave in order to take on the necessary job, on safari in Kenya or buying ponies in Iceland. As usual she lacked his presence, and wrote:

> Only now, when the fields stretch out between the ears of your horse – only now, while you are drinking beer with alien maidens – the sweet love of your wife comes back to you. . . .
> . . . I have my dark hours, hours of being doomed, victim of myself. No escape from that. Sometimes I feel that all I touch and intend to do turns into mist and vapour, withers away; all I do seems half done, ill done, corrupt, confused. And it hurts. I would like to be proud of myself – everyone needs to feel that things can grow under his hand, that he can plant or heal or build or fashion outer or inner life; everyone needs to feel that he can, if he will, be strong and brave and pure, even though he takes his time, even though the moment is rare, the time unripe. But I am always like a vine without a stick, and I am always in two minds, divided, and therefore the easiest way comes first. . . . These thoughts are the dead fruits of conscious regrets. My Tree tonight is heavy with them. . . .

Sometimes, however, she was able to join him abroad and her spirits would soar straight away. On one occasion, at a smart stag hunt in France, he found her a good mount and she had luckily brought over her riding clothes but lacked the appropriate headgear. He told her not to worry, and went on ahead. They found quickly, and during a check one of the followers came up to him and said, 'What an elegant hat your wife is wearing!' Friedrich turned round and saw that Iris was sporting a jaunty black stocking-cap embroidered with a scarlet 'L', which he did not immediately recognize as one of his own shoe bags.

The Rainbow Picnic

A few weeks later, while waiting for the Oranmores at the Hotel Crillon in Paris, she wrote to him:

I am often very unhappy. I think I have not got an American Halloween pumpkin smile upon my soul. . . . Elegant restaurants seem sometimes like torture-chambers.

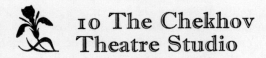

10 The Chekhov Theatre Studio

During her sojourn in Ireland Iris wrote several plays and though she herself realized they were not up to professional standard, the mere achievement encouraged her to persevere. She was eager to acquire more knowledge and experience, and so she and Friedrich decided to join the Chekhov Theatre Studio in Devonshire, he as an actor, she as a writer.

Michael Chekhov, a nephew of the dramatist, was already a hero figure to Iris, although she had not yet clapped eyes on him. But while staying at the Seven Stars Hotel in Totnes before moving into the Theatre Studio premises just outside the town, she got to know him well by sight. Despite all her efforts to meet him, however, no encounter occurred until one day, at Totnes Station, he offered to carry her battered suitcase, which burst open and strewed the platform with a rainbow fall of crumpled garments and beads.

Chekhov believed in permeating the body with the mood of the matter it was trying to express. He considered the physical approach to acting more important than mind and memory, and had therefore devised certain movements which all his students – the writers and musicians as well as the actors – were required to perform. Iris could read a poem better than any of them, but often became awkward with embarrassment when doing these exercises. However, she loved the spirit of dedication that Chekhov instilled – 'the theatre is your church' – and enjoyed wearing the long blue smock which he had decreed as the student uniform. His little community lived in perfect harmony and idyllic circumstances, comfortably installed at Rednorth House, a large mansion built for Isadora Duncan by one of her rich lovers (but never inhabited by her), with beautiful gardens and, incidentally, a first-rate chef.

This happy and fruitful period of Iris's life was soon interrupted, however, by her mother's death. The cinema had enhanced Lady Tree's last years. She had enjoyed playing character parts in films and had developed a passion for Sir Alexander Korda, to whom she always coyly referred as 'he who shall remain nameless'. Meanwhile she had still delighted in making puns. When her lawyer came to see her about her will, she had said: 'Ah, I suppose you've come to teach me my death duties.'

'It was all very shocking and terrible,' Iris wrote to Maud, 'but death gave back for an instant all the beauty of life, and there was nothing but flowers left. . . . Viola and Felicity were very sweet and tremendously efficient and I felt very near to them both. . . . We went to Brancaster. . . .'

To all three sisters Brancaster recalled memories of happy childhood. To Viola it was also associated, more poignantly, with her husband Alan, for it was here that she had fallen in love with him at first sight, had later become secretly engaged to him and, later still, in the first years of their marriage, spent many a golden day with him and the children, 'dabbing for flat fish with a trident and in a tawny skirt, a hank of hair bound with blue . . . looking not unlike Britannia on a penny'.*

One day, two years after her mother's death, Viola found – to her surprise, since it was her favourite dish – that she could not face the dressed crab she had ordered. She was not conscious of having felt ill, yet from that moment she went into a decline. Iris wrote to her from Les Baux where she was on holiday with Friedrich:

---

* Viola Tree, 'Dabbing', article published in the *Star*.

The Chekhov Theatre Studio

I hope you are better. I burnt a tall white candle for you in such a beautiful church in Marseille by a great figure of Christ whose feet the peasants kissed. All white-haired women dressed in black; the markets and the fish pleased me well; pleased again with the masts of ships behind and with the saffron fish soup and wine and the comfortable excited foreigners. . . .

Friedrich is very nice with a fine car and looking beautiful as always; I am glad to be with him again and here, on the heights of a robber king's great castle, stony and wild overlooking the valley of olives. I was here with him before Boon, hiding him from Diana – do you remember?

Oh get well soon. I love you so!

But when she got back to England she found her sister was no better.

'Viola, do you believe there is going to be an after life?' she asked her.

Viola smiled: 'There'll always be "merrily, merrily under the blossom that hangs on the bough".'

Early in 1939, after several months in hospital, she died. Stricken, Iris returned to the Chekhov Theatre Studio and immersed herself in work.

Since the establishment was financed by an American woman, Beatrice Streaight, many of the students came from the United States. One of them was a little girl of twelve called Daphne, whom Iris came across one day behind the rose bushes weeping with disappointment at not being allowed, on account of her age, to attend a performance of the Ballet Joos. To cheer her up, she drew her into a discussion about Shakespeare's plays and, as the child (now Mrs Field) in later life stated,* 'I soon forgot all about Joos and started on probably the most influential friendship of my life'.

With the clouds of war gathering in Europe, Beatrice Streaight decided to move the Studio to America, and by the summer of 1939 had installed it, with all its students, in a large

---

*In a letter to the author.

country house surrounded by woods and lakes near Ridgefield, Connecticut. Here, shortly afterwards, she found herself involved in a romantic liaison with Friedrich.

To Iris, Friedrich's temporary defection was to a certain extent mitigated by her own affection for a member of the staff, Alan Harkness, a dedicated teacher, a devotee of the theatre, a vegetarian and a pacifist, an idealist who never lacked courage in defending his beliefs. He and Iris complemented each other; her sense of fun brightened his gravity and ignited his humour, while his admiration and encouragement of her writing spurred her on to further efforts. But, as she explained in a letter to Maud Russell:

> I am at times discouraged (like all the other students) with work and being caged – but I like the contented life really and the bells ringing for lectures, discussions and food.
> Private life is apt to spread so – sometimes into sloughs and sometimes into mazes, and to find the perfect adjustment needs so much firmness and fierce will.
> I have so often planned a perfect day in my head and it seems simple, but then one misses out an essential of which one is unaware or an accident which we cannot prefigure. The Truth – so much of the charm of life, depends on chance encounter, on novelty, on odd association and however much one thinks 'I will read, exercise, write, think, sleep, concentrate, eat more fruit, learn the harp', one is forfeiting the absolute nourishment and avoiding perhaps the ultimate necessity to love, laugh and perhaps to suffer; I see this among the students – they get so depressed at times simply because they have to live together in a beautiful country house with a lake and woods, leaving the art they chose under the guidance of a great genius with twenty-five intelligent young people, every creature comfort and a good Chinese cook – What other leaven is necessary? Freedom? We know freedom – What then, Strife? Something perhaps intensely personal like a latch-key or a vice? Anyway 'happiness' – the rosy-yellow infinity that all men dream is hard to find except at moments. I find it often at moments – And you?

The Chekhov Theatre Studio

For the holidays Iris rented a little cottage at Martha's Vineyard, where Alan Harkness and Daphne came and joined her and Boon. On the isolated beach Alan and the two children, all stark naked, would smear their bodies with grey clay and leap around like Red Indians performing a war-dance before racing, whooping, into the waves. But Iris went swimming alone, for, although her body was still beautiful and white as a lily, she was shy of exposing it to others.

Here she began to take an enjoyment in cooking, inventing original dishes, including *Figues Iris* – layers of sliced green figs alternating with red currant jelly, topped with cream and finally sprinkled with grated bitter chocolate. An apple pie baking in the oven was to her a symbol of hearth and home, while kedgeree reminded her of her mother's breakfasts, just as two boiled eggs for tea after bathing brought back memories of Brancaster. On wet days she made toffee and marzipan as she had done when she was still in the schoolroom.

From Martha's Vineyard she again wrote to Maud:

Another sea-side, another summer sand and smell. A holiday from my Chekhov School and came to this island with Boon – partly because I liked the name and it is very lovely, 30 miles long with different kinds of landscapes and beaches, one boisterous, one calm, one hilly and pondy, one with thick woods; the gentry's gallant colonial houses with honeysuckle gardens or wooden shacks like mine or villages with buoys and near yachts. My shack has no light, water, servant, village or car. But I have blueberries and a dozen eggs – that ought to go a long way and the ice-man brought ice. We are on the shore, great bouncing waves in front with wild rose wilderness and ponds behind – real; as usual I sacrificed comfort and company for romance, since we are miles away from the summer gentry, including Pearl Buck, and much of the writing time is spent on meals, washing up, amusing Boon, and the sea.

When the next term started, Chekhov commissioned Iris to write a play for children. With Alan's help she produced a witty entertainment, *Sing About It*, introducing all kinds of

The Rainbow Picnic

ballads, from *The Raggle Taggle Gipsies* down to *Frankie and Johnnie*. It was a tremendous success and encouraged her and Alan to collaborate on other plays. Their partnership was short-lived. When America entered the war, many of the students were drafted and the Theatre Studio eventually closed down.

Iris then moved to California and rented a house in the beautiful Ojai Valley ('Peace Nest' to the Indians, Shangri-la in the original film version of *Lost Horizon*), with a sunset view of mountains rising in transparent layers like a Japanese painting. Here she and Boon settled in with two white Alsatian dogs, Lupa and Dingo, a black goat called Nuba and a white one named Amaryllis from a poem which began:

> In the days of daffodillies
> Went the white goat Amaryllis....

She also kept a gaggle of geese, known as 'the peep-peeps', which she used to cradle in her arms, warming herself against their soft feathered bodies.

A near neighbour was the Indian sage, Krishnamurti, whose lectures she often attended. In this mystical aspect of her nature she took after her Aunt Dora, who had become a Sister of Mercy after leading an extremely worldly life. No ordinary nun, she had written the words of an army marching song which, with her Mother Superior's permission, was published anonymously. The chorus went like this:

> Left right, left right,
> The girl that I left
> Is the girl that is right.

Her brother Max, with whom she spent many holidays in Italy, delighted in her company. Sitting on the terrace of his villa at Rapallo, he would help her choose the colours and materials she used for her patchwork quilts; together they would solve crossword puzzles and play paper games. After her last visit, before her death in 1940, she wrote to him from her convent cell: 'My thoughts are with you, how I envy my thoughts!'

In due course Iris was joined at Ojai by Alan Harkness and

Daphne. Round them gathered a dozen former Chekhov students who converted the local schoolhouse into a theatre and thus formed the nucleus of a repertory company which eventually opened with a play by Iris called *Second Wind*.

Happy and creative days ensued. The war was nearly over. Friedrich's liaison with Beatrice Streaight had been brought to an end by her marriage to a political journalist and he reappeared at regular intervals. Ivan, after being brought up as an English schoolboy at Dartington, was now serving as an American officer in the Signal Corps and turned up on leave. Boon was going to a school in the valley, from which he eventually took a scholarship to Harvard. The atmosphere, as Daphne Field recalls, was one of 'relaxed joy. . . . We did some experiments with improvising and Iris wrote a play from the improvisations. Nothing came of that particular experiment, but these are the things you try when life is slowed down the right way.'

One of Iris's ideas which did bear fruit, however, was the Ojai Festival, for which the group produced *Macbeth*. An established actor, Ford Rainey, played the name part and Iris herself appeared as Lady Macbeth. No one had thought of her before as an actress, but she gave a magnificent performance, even though her stage fright was immeasurably increased by the presence in the audience of her friends Lillian Gish, Charlie Chaplin and Greta Garbo.

For some time the group was without a manager, since Alan Harkness now married one of the female members and went off with her to live in Switzerland. Meanwhile, with financial help from Friedrich, Iris and Ford bought an apricot ranch, which they ran together while continuing to put on plays. But they soon found it impossible to combine agriculture with art, and the group would have again dissolved had not Harkness and his wife returned to breathe new life into it. From then on it went from strength to strength, for, as Daphne Field asserts,

> Iris was good for Ford as an actor. She was good for all of us in that way. Never satisfied, always wanting it more excit-

ing. Never settling for the easy way out even up to the moment of the curtain, which would sometimes send us crazy. She is the one person who could never have made the compromise to have a commercial career and she was genuinely bored with anything but artistic success.

In addition to the ranch, Iris also acquired a barn by the sea on an estate that had once belonged to Robert Louis Stevenson's family. Here she gave Sunday brunches and dinners for over a hundred guests at a time – no mean feat for someone reputed to be a bad housekeeper – and, as Daphne Field recalled, 'she had a way of making *rocolto* sound like something fantastic and grandly offer Mr Simon's wine (which wasn't any better than any other cheap Californian wine, but you had been with Iris and shared her delight in the Italian family which made it) and it became something special.'

As a hide-out for herself and Ford, she discovered yet a third residence: an apartment built over a merry-go-round on the Santa Monica pier, which she was unable to resist.

But these joys were of short duration. Soon afterwards Alan Harkness, who was learning to drive, stalled his engine while crossing the railway track and was killed by an oncoming train. This tragedy put an end to the group. Shortly afterwards Ford Rainey, who had meanwhile fallen in love with a younger woman, went away to marry her, and although Iris had known all along that this might happen, she suffered. To add to her sorrow, she also heard that her gallant Swiss captain, Eric Meiville, had fallen in battle, fighting for the Finns. Grieving, she wrote a poem for a commemoratory stone to be placed at Castle MacGarret, the place he had loved most on earth:

> This is autumn, this is bare. . . .
> Let the spring throw all its sweetness on the air,
> Let the green earth bud.
> Winter comes through and the snow that sucked his blood –
> That jaunty figure, boastful, trim,
> The horseman, hunter, lover, clown
> And the best fighter, so soon down.

> Empty clothes, empty saddles, empty glass,
> Riderless the horses pass
> And the women who have no sons
> Must pray themselves to sleep like nuns.

But not a bit of it: the captain, as she later learnt, had survived without a scratch, to ride more horses, fill many another glass, and meet her again.

Meanwhile she herself was in a bad way. The apricot farm had been sold at a loss, which, as she put it, 'cooked my hash', and she wrote in desperation to Friedrich:

> Last dollar in telephone box. . . . We must make our lives clearer and straighter; we must plan better. I must have a home for Boon. Perhaps I could have three husbands, you only one wife. How would that be?

11 The Glass Bubble

In spite of her long absence in America, on returning to Europe after the war Iris was immediately able to pick up the threads of her former life since she had kept in touch with all her friends by assiduous correspondence. One of her first ports of call was Paris, where Duff Cooper had just been appointed British Ambassador, and where she was now warmly welcomed into the little court of intellect and beauty that had gathered round Diana and Duff in the *salon vert* at the Embassy.

Another favourite of Diana's, but a stranger to Iris, was Louise de Vilmorin, the well-known writer, a lovely, elegant and witty woman, with many charming mannerisms and affectations.*

She would enter a room with a slight dramatic limp, making an almost imperceptible pause on the threshold, one long-fingered hand held against her heart, her lips half parted and her eyes wide and shining. Her style of dress was studiously romantic and vaguely Hungarian† in conception, consisting of short jewel-coloured velvet jackets trimmed with sable or mink, black skirts and white blouses, and embroidered neck ribbons. In the daytime her dark chestnut-coloured hair was arranged in a plaited chignon tied with a velvet bow; at night she wore it brushed

---

* She signed her letters and poems with a four-leafed clover drawn in one flowing line.
† The nationality of her first husband, Count Palfy.

The Glass Bubble

up from her forehead, pinned back with diamond stars, and falling loosely down her back in the fashion of the Empress Elisabeth of Austria. Her long evening dresses were made of floating gossamer-like material. For big occasions she wore a magnificent parure of aquamarines and pearls.

In comparison, Iris sometimes felt as tawdry as a fairy off the top of last year's Christmas tree. Clothes had always caused her a great deal of worry. Owning no conventional wardrobe, she resorted to improvisation, dressing in a manner appropriate to her legend. Sometimes her efforts misfired and she would then become embarrassed and shy. Inevitably, in the circumstances, she failed to hit it off with Louise. They were like two rival actresses sharing the lead on the same playbill, both accustomed to carry the audience, neither ceding a single laurel leaf to the other. Iris did not enjoy listening to Louise declaiming French poetry, singing ballads and accompanying herself on the guitar; while Louise was unable to appreciate Iris's play on words, spontaneous clowning or mimicry.

The person Iris missed most of all on her return to England was Curtis; for meanwhile he had gone back to America. And there, in 1949, he died. Although they had not met for years, she was afflicted by his sudden death and stricken with remorse. She felt she was to blame for the shipwreck of their marriage, and the pangs of guilt that assailed her were all the sharper since her marriage to Friedrich had likewise come to grief and was presently to end in divorce.

One of her favourite European capitals was what she called 'fountaining Rome' and here, though hardly knowing how or why, she found herself installed for a time in 'my glass bubble', a one-room apartment at the top of a building overlooking the Spanish Steps, eight floors up, with no lift, no heating, but with a glassed-in balcony affording a splendid view. Though small, uncomfortable and inconvenient, it was undeniably romantic and imbued with her personality: her little equestrian portrait by Carrington rested against a pile of books on the table; a chart of mushrooms, given to her by Boon, hung on the wall; roughly cured sheepskins were thrown over the chairs; and two silver chalices stood on a small chest together with her amber beads, chunks of turquoise and Friedrich's antique silver belt.

In these confined surroundings space had to be found not only for herself but also for Aguri, the large black Belgian sheepdog she had recently acquired: a sweet-tempered and devoted animal with exceptional intelligence – he understood perfectly the private multi-lingual jargon in which she addressed him – but with a voracious appetite and extremely expensive to feed. And since she was as usual in financial straits, when it came to the crunch she sacrificed herself for him and went without lunch or dinner. When Maud Russell came to see her on a brief visit, she noticed Iris had lost her appetite almost completely and was able to eat next to nothing, her stomach having shrunk as a result of skipping so many meals. But even when a windfall did arrive, in the shape of a cheque from England or America, Iris preferred to spend the money on expensive face creams rather than on food for herself, in the hope of removing the cobweb-like network of lines that now veiled her white skin. (She economized, however, on her hair by washing and cutting it herself, then rinsing it with tea to preserve its red-gold colour.)

One of the advantages of living in Rome was that it enabled her to see more of her uncle Max, who had retired many years ago in Rapallo, having 'deliberately brought his life to a standstill'* at the age of forty. She would find him sitting on his terrace, as elegant as ever in a pearl-grey suit, with a straw boater cocked forward over his eyes, and one of his own gardenias in his buttonhole.

On her last visit, in March 1954, he was eighty-three years old and dying. 'You are very much loved, Uncle Max,' she said impulsively, 'everyone loves you.' A look of pleasure came into his fading eyes. 'Well, my dear,' he answered, with an effort, 'I was always – er – a well-wisher.'†

In Rome, as everywhere else, Iris found herself surrounded by friends. Jenny Nicholson, the journalist daughter of Robert Graves, and her husband Patrick Crosse, the Reuters correspondent, were cronies of long standing. Through them she met

* David Cecil, *op. cit.*
† *Ibid.*

The Glass Bubble

two younger colleagues, David Kelly and Nigel Ryan. There was also Judy Montagu, soon to be married to the art historian Milton Gendell, who lived on an island in the middle of the Tiber. Derek Hill, Director of the British School, introduced her to his students, on whom she made an unforgettable impression when, at a poetry reading, dressed in cloth of gold on the candlelit stage, she delivered 'Tiger, tiger, burning bright....'

Nevertheless she was sometimes lonely and vented her nostalgia in letters addressed now to the younger generation of her family. To her nephew David Parsons, a pig breeder and spare-time writer, who helped her financially when he could, she wrote:

> I am often troubled with the sweets of memory, wishing to puff back the loveliest days and put them together with the good days now — what a crowd: Felicity at every age, Daddy in all his best parts, Viola singing through all her ranges. That is one's primitive hope of Heaven. But it will all be in one clear drop, in essence perhaps.

And again:

> On reading the 230 pages of my novel which I just raced along with, I find that most of it has to go out — most of it has a sad surprise of disappointment. But perhaps with a lot of loin-girding I can make it into something. It's awfully gloomy... *tant pis.*

This novel never came to anything, but she did have a number of her poems published in *Botteghe Oscure* and succeeded in getting her play *Strangers' Wharf* put on at the New Lindsey Theatre in London. She made a flying visit to England in order to attend the first night and through her usual unpunctuality nearly missed the start of the performance. She was gratified next day, however, by the favourable reviews, notably that of *The Times*:

> If anyone were able to revive the forgotten art of melodrama it would surely be the daughter of Sir Herbert Tree. *Strangers' Wharf*, by Miss Iris Tree, deserves to be seen as a

> theatrical curiosity, for here in miniature the mechanism of the old art has been set ticking into motion once again: and it is a mechanism which, for all its preposterousness, works upon the stage.
>
> The few characters are all phantoms conjured out of the property basket. They float into the junk shop of a Caribbean seaport, a hovel strewn with fishing nets, gewgaws, and faded clothes. Among them is a pretty orphan in white, virtually imprisoned in the shop by the wretched hag who owns it. Her father, a rich Englishman, who collects watches, returns to the island to visit her mother's grave and is murdered by a drunken lounger. The plot hardly matters; the dialogue is nearly always crude, but the play holds the stage by an instinct for construction, and it manages to work up many old ingredients — oaths and scuffles, a hidden letter, a walking ghost, a melancholy ship's horn, and even a dream — into an attractively thick brew.

During this visit she went and stayed with her niece Virginia, now married to Henry Bath and living at Job's Mill, near Warminster, to whom she subsequently wrote:

> It was splendid to meet England again at its loveliest trysting place, in its loveliest month and to find you by your mill stream nesting like two swans.

Shortly afterwards Virginia became pregnant and Iris felt partly responsible; for it was she who had suggested and indeed conducted her and Henry on a pilgrimage to the Cerne Giant, a vast figure in full phallic splendour carved out of the chalk hillside at Cerne Abbas, to whom, according to local legend, any woman wishing for a child should pay her respects. In due course Virginia's daughter was appropriately christened Silvy Cerne.

Meanwhile Friedrich had remarried and had a son by his second wife. Iris was never able to reconcile herself to this, for she could still hardly believe she was divorced from him. She continued to regard him as her husband and to write to him, confiding her innermost thoughts:

The Glass Bubble

For poets of life like you and me, it's impossible. We will have to suffer, like veterans of war, the loss of limbs and sight. We will have to leap and fall, run and tumble, to the grave – there is no other way. . . . But there is a way when we are free of cravings and anxious machinations, when we refuse to win, leave the arena – then all the glory, the joy of leaves brushing us in the chase, the splash of water, the flight of wind will take us and lift us beyond memory into a new freedom.

By this time Friedrich was an established film actor and, since he was mostly employed by the Italian director Fellini, his work often brought him to Rome. Iris, too, was given a part in one of Fellini's films, *La Dolce Vita*, in which she appeared as herself, reading poetry as she had often done at Genet de Margerie's Roman salon. In this scene all the other guests drift away and leave her reading on alone. When a friend later asked her why she had taken such an unflattering part, she opened her eyes in amazement: 'For the lolly, of course!'

The 'lolly' enabled her to travel to other parts of Italy. Thus in Venice, rounding a street corner, she came face to face with her old friend and rival Nancy Cunard, whom she had not seen for over thirty years. Nancy was still dressed in her original style: a turban of multi-coloured string netting wound round her head; a high fur collar framing her small pale face; her massive African bracelets of ebony and ivory clattering together on her now bony arms; her eyes outlined in shiny black like a Van Dongen model, but now faded to a paler blue like sea-glass bleached by salt water. But instead of her erstwhile stiletto-heeled shoes she wore plimsolls, having taken a tumble off a mule in Capri.

In Venice I, too, met Iris again after more than twenty years. It was on a rainy day, in a little trattoria where I was lunching with my husband Xan. Suddenly she made her appearance, wearing a Galloway skirt of scarlet flannel, a black tabard and, for want of a better word to describe her headgear, a 'runcible hat' which appeared to be made of thick translucent india-rubber jelly set in a hat-shaped mould. At her heels, a black familiar, was Aguri. Both of them were dripping wet.

Ischia was another haunt of hers, for she revelled in the local radioactive baths and spent many a blissful moment buried up to her neck in the hot health-giving waters. Here, as everywhere else, she searched for a cabin or scrap of land on which to build a shack, and even toyed with the idea of living in one of the bleached white caves scooped out of the salt-covered rocks as though by a giant spoon. For a time she actually did rent a peasant house, consisting of two whitewashed rooms – no ordinary dwelling, as she discovered to her delight; for the surrounding vegetation was gargantuan and, though she knew this was due to a mineral content in the soil and water which caused everything to grow like Jack's beanstalk, she preferred to regard it as the result of a magic spell.

The 'lolly' from her part in *La Dolce Vita* had also enabled her to buy a second-hand car: an enormous Alfa-Romeo that had belonged to a Roman princeling. It was caddish in appearance, a glutton for petrol, and as hard to control as an unbroken horse. For an impoverished middle-aged lady who had not driven for years, no vehicle could have been less suitable; and Iris was frankly, and justifiably, terrified of it. With her usual audacity, however, she headed out of Rome on yet another jaunt to Ischia. By some miracle she reached Naples safe and sound, and, since she would not be needing a car on the island, left the monster with a sigh of relief in a garage down by the docks. On returning from her holiday some weeks later she found, where the garage had been, only a large hole in the ground. There was no sign of her car and, since she had left the log-book and all the other papers in the glove-box, no proof that she had ever owned it. She got back to Rome by train.

One summer she went even further afield, invited by Diana to join a party of friends on the *Eros*, a yacht lent by Niarchos. 'We will tour the wilder Greek isles,' she wrote to Virginia. 'The *Eros* is beautiful and graceful, black with white masts, and very luxurious.'

At the suggestion of Paddy Leigh Fermor, who was one of the party, the cruise included a visit to the Mani, the central prong of the Peloponnese, one of the least known and most beautiful parts of the Mediterranean. Iris's pulse raced with excitement as they neared the shore and she saw the sky-line pricked with ruined towers over which her imagination circled like a bird questing for a nesting-place. On landing she wandered off in search of a solitary beach on which to bathe by herself while the others went for a walk. On their way back they looked over the edge of a cliff and saw, far below, floating in a creek, a body lily-white against the wine-dark sea – a derelict nymph indeed.

12 Personal View of Iris

By the early 1960s Iris had left Rome and reverted to her nomadic life. Boon in the meantime had married, sired a son, been divorced, remarried, sired two more children and was now studying medicine in Geneva with his second wife, a beautiful Polish girl named Ilona, who was likewise a medical student. Iris therefore had an additional reason for visiting Switzerland, a country she loved, and from Gstaad, on a lovely day in June, she wrote to Virginia:

> Here I am in the almost too green slopes of these mountains, with a neat wood-smelling apartment in a chalet. Cream flows like wine, and wine flows like waterfalls, and everything is smooth and clean, running on well-ordered wheels, with a toy train to bring the tiny world here, but really it's quite large.
> Krishnamurti talks with wonderful clarity and inspiration, hard and sharp and eventual. The Huxleys were here for a week or more, excellent – we dined together and walked. Boon and Ilona came on Saturday and return tomorrow with Marius, my cowboy grandson. Menuhin gives concerts on 18th for 2 weeks so I think I shall stay. I can't pull myself up by my espadrille straps now. . . . I may go to Paris to follow on Krishnamurti's talks there. Meanwhile I am nearish to

Boon in Geneva. Perhaps you will come here for mountain air and cream? It's really rather ripping.

She liked Gstaad just as much in the winter, even though she did not ski since she suffered from fear of heights. One afternoon Costa Achillopoulos, the Greek photographer, skiing through a wood above the village, came across her trudging through the snow – a hallucinatory figure, tall, pale and gaunt, wrapped in a dark green cloak with a hood pulled over her head, and followed by a big black dog. He had never seen Iris before and in the gathering dusk, with snow beginning to fall, he wondered whether this was not a phantom he had conjured out of his own imagination. That evening, however, he found she was indeed flesh and blood, when he met her at the inn with Patrick and Jenny Crosse and Robert Graves. Subsequently, from the higher slopes on which he spent every day, he would glimpse her now and then in the valley below, a lone figure outlined against the snow, accompanied by her familiar.

Her wanderings during this period took her back to Languedoc and Provence, where she joined her friends, Paddy Leigh Fermor, Joan Rayner and Dorothy Lygon. With them, in the marshlands of the Camargue, among black bulls, she rode a white horse again. On a visit to Aigues-Mortes, as she was crossing the Place Saint-Louis, she called out:

'Come and see, there's a statue of me here!'

And indeed the bronze effigy of the canonized crusader king closely resembled her in features, style and stance.

In the autumn of 1962 she was back in London for a while and Penelope Smail, Curtis's daughter by his second wife, invited her to meet Richard Morphet, of the Tate Gallery, before going on to his flat to see her portrait by Vanessa Bell which he now owned. Morphet later recalled:

It was a wildly windy, blustery day with aerated rain. Tim and Penelope Smail and I waited for almost an hour in their house at 7 Moore Street for Iris Tree to arrive, and she was so late that we were just setting off without her when she came.... She had just left her Rome flat, high up at the top of long steps, and doesn't know where she will live next, Spain perhaps. She arrived on foot. . . . Before I saw her I heard her: 'It's so beautiful walking through dead leaves' came floating up the stairs in her deep voice. . . . She walked into the room carrying a sheaf of yellow flowers and two red roses and she thrust these like a stick at Penelope, in an erratic, almost doll-like but very graceful movement. She wore a blue suit, the top half like a shirt, with a vivid orange/yellow silk scarf at the neck, shiny black leather shoes, and a bag over her shoulder on a strap. In a long striding walk, she approached the sofa and sat down on it in one quick movement, curling her feet under her. After about a minute . . . she began combing her straight yellow hair as she talked, and went on combing it for some minutes. She said she was glad she had had her children far apart (ten years): otherwise it was inevitable for a parent to have a favourite. . . .

She spoke longingly of world peace and with tremendous admiration of Bertrand Russell's efforts, and said she wished for a great upsurge of American and Russian youth together in a movement to defy war. She spoke of the Russian nuclear missiles in Cuba as 'cannons'.

She admired, spontaneously, almost everything she saw, walked round the room looking at things, itemizing them verbally to herself as she walked — 'beautiful door . . . logs . . . books . . . bottle,' etc. Also whenever anyone said anything, she would often repeat, verbatim, exactly what they had just said. She did this, so to speak, in the abstract — not, apparently, either conversationally or as something consciously spoken to herself. . . .

She was engaged on her autobiography, but held up, she said, by absence of total recall and dislike of the type of dramatic passage and revelations which characterize so many autobiographies; what she remembered most clearly were her emotional relationships, and she had no wish to lay them bare.

When her home had been in Calfornia, at a time when she was away in Europe, all her papers had been lost. They included her diaries, letters from Ivan in the war, and letters

Personal View of Iris

from her parents. They were simply put in the rubbish bin. She was heartbroken. We discussed Aldous Huxley's similar recent fate. . . . His papers, which also included manuscripts and unprinted family papers going back over generations, had gone up in flames before his eyes when *his* California house was burnt. He just managed to rescue the manuscript of his most recent novel. It was especially ironic, Iris said, that the fire had started in the lower part of the house which was occupied by another couple; the Huxleys, assured that it would be contained there, energetically helped the occupants to get their stuff out. . . . Another link between Iris and Aldous Huxley was that she too had taken mescalin. . . . She also admired very deeply and affectionately Curtis Moffat's photographs (which have great stylistic affinities with some of [Man] Ray's work).*

When they got to Morphet's flat 'her greatest delight was my kaleidoscope. Through it she gazed enraptured, making noises, at the Surf packet, at Pomona, at targets and Union Jacks, at a mug full of pencils, and above all at her own eyes painted by Vanessa Bell. This will remain perhaps my definitive image of her, peering, as through a telescope but at point blank range, at these beautiful shapes in two shades of blue which were her own eyes. . . .'

Though Iris still had no permanent mooring anywhere, she was increasingly attracted to the little fishing port of Cadaques on the Costa Brava, which was unfashionable but frequented by what she called 'corduroys': impoverished artists and intellectuals dressed in 'rag, tag and bobtails' like herself. Meanwhile, thanks to a cheque from Ivan – part of his 'filmgotten gains' – she had acquired another second-hand car, a little blue beetle of a Volkswagen. New highways opened up before her, fresh picnic grounds beckoned, and distant friends became more accessible.

Thus she set out to join Diana who had come to stay with us in Portugal. We were expecting Iris to arrive on a certain day. When she failed to turn up we began to grow anxious. But at last, at three o'clock in the afternoon, a telephone call

---

* Excerpts from Richard Morphet's personal diary, 20 October 1962.

The Rainbow Picnic

came through. Iris, it appeared, was stranded on the road just this side of the frontier.

'I might have known it,' said Diana. 'Not a penny on her, not a word of the language, and her car has broken down. But, trust her, she's already found a knight errant. They've just had lunch together and he's going to bring her here in his own car straight away. And – can you beat it? – it seems he's a diamond merchant!'

Iris turned up in triumph that evening in a large limousine, with her diamond merchant at the wheel, her guardian-wolf sitting in the back, and her luggage (mostly dog food) in the boot.

To have either Iris or Diana as a guest was a rewarding experience. To have them both staying together was a perpetual and stimulating entertainment. The curtain of the day would be raised by Diana's early morning cry of 'Are you awake, doll?' delivered in that characteristic flat tone of hers, followed by Iris's initial grunt of annoyance at being woken so early. A long conversation would ensue, consisting of brilliant repartee and sounding all the more ribald and uninhibited for being carried on at the tops of their voices as they shouted to each other from their respective rooms.

This verbal duel would continue intermittently throughout the day, punctuated by a chortle from one or the other as a thrust went home or a point was scored. From time to time Iris would get down to work on the long poem she was writing – I often watched her sitting in the window seat in her vividly striped Mexican poncho, her head bent over her copy-book, absorbed in composition – or go out into the garden to throw sticks for Aguri, shouting 'Bèllo boy! Bèllo boy!' and patting him as he retrieved and delivered in style. At other moments she would burst into song and I was sometimes surprised to hear *The Boys Dressed in Blue*, an American Civil War song, rendered in *basso profundo* tones and a pronounced Austrian accent, as she affectionately imitated Friedrich's voice.

In due course her blue beetle was repaired and delivered to our house. On her last evening with us we all went out to dine in a restaurant on the coast. Here, her puns became more and more outrageous and, with typical prodigality, she lavished them even on the uncomprehending waiter. 'Shall I Campari to a summer's day?' she murmured as he set her apéritif before her. She continued in this vein throughout the meal, highlighting her performance with actions to suit her words. 'What's that fish you're eating?' she enquired of Xan.

'I don't know what it's called in English,' he replied, 'but in Portuguese it's *cherne* – spelled C-H-E-R-N-E and pronounced "share'n".'

'Share'n share alike, then,' said she, spearing a morsel off his plate and handing him a sardine on the end of her fork.

Next morning she headed back to Cadaques to 'paste a broken house together with vinegar and brown paper'. Luckily for Xan and me, we knew we would be seeing her again in a few weeks' time since we had been invited by some friends to stay there over Christmas.

The 'broken house' proved to be most ingeniously pasted together, but very short on furniture and household equipment. Iris by herself could easily have made do with only three rickety chairs, two bowls, two mugs and some bent cutlery; but Boon, Ilona and their two infants had come from Geneva for the holidays and were also staying there. What with these additional inmates and the Christmas tree, there was scarcely room to move. Nevertheless, with borrowed glasses and drinks on credit, she gave a party for a dozen guests to celebrate Boon's recent achievement in passing his final exams.

By this time she had established herself as a local celebrity, almost on a par with her friend Salvador Dali who lived in the bay round the corner, and she held court every day at Meliton's in preference to any other café, chiefly because she was intrigued by the owner, a handsome white-haired Catalan, who was said to have had a romantic past as a smuggler. I came across her here one morning surrounded by a number of cronies admiring her latest hat: a brown woollen Balaclava helmet she had found on a beach-combing expedition the evening before.

Her evening togs were equally eccentric, but more elegant. At another party, given in an antique shop, she wore a Nattier-blue velvet smoking jacket with satin facings that had once

The Rainbow Picnic

belonged to Duff Cooper, and a huge pink Malmaison carnation in her button-hole. Later on, when the band started up, she accompanied in mime, drawing an imaginary bow across the strings of a notional violin – and looking so like a figure in a Chagall painting that I almost expected to see a green goat dancing on its hind legs beside her among the grandfather clocks and rocking chairs.

On our last evening we were sitting with her outside Meliton's waiting for that magic hour *entre chien et loup* which Thomas Hardy called 'the pinking in of the day', when she sprang to her feet and said: 'Quick! Let's go to Rosas. It'll be even better there.'

We drove fast over the hills to the neighbouring harbour, racing the sinking sun, and arrived just before it sank in a flood of red-gold light. As we stood watching it disappear, the fishing fleet came chugging into port. 'Like beating hearts. . . .' With a blissful expression on her face, Iris repeated the words and then, as though having tasted them and found them adequate, recited the rest of the line she had just composed:

'When boats like beating hearts come home. . . .'

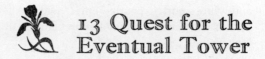

13 Quest for the Eventual Tower

The next time we saw Iris was in France, for by then we had left Portugal and were living in a rented farmhouse north of Uzès while looking for somewhere permanent to settle. The severe stone building stood some distance away from a semi-abandoned hamlet in the middle of unpopulated moorlands, and looked so isolated and windblown that we had instinctively named it 'Wuthering Heights'. Since there was no one within miles of whom one could ask the way, it was extremely difficult to find. One evening in late autumn I heard a tap on the glass terrace door and discerned a tall cloaked figure standing outside. Then a familiar peal of laughter rang out and Iris entered, followed by Aguri.

'I'm looking for an eventual tower,' she announced. 'I heard you were house-hunting too, and thought we may as well join forces.'

And so she moved in. We helped her to unload the little blue beetle and I noticed there was now an addition to her personal possessions: a pen-and-ink outline of her own hand traced and charted by a fortune-teller. I was not surprised to see that her heart ruled her head, and found myself again admiring her eloquent witty hands – 'palms of glee', as Nancy Cunard had called them.*

* Nancy Cunard, *Sublunary* (Hodder and Stoughton, 1923).

The Rainbow Picnic

I also noticed a Dick Whittington bundle, a bulging red-and-white spotted handkerchief, which she handled as gingerly as if it contained a valuable porcelain or some precious archaeological find.

'What have you got there?' I asked.

'Ah ha! A surprise, something rare and strange.'

'Animal, vegetable or mineral?'

'Vegetable. *Now* can you guess?'

'Mushrooms!'

'Absolutely right, but not in the plural. This is *one* mushroom, a very special kind of mushroom, a *hallucinogenous* mushroom, producing beatific visions in glorious Technicolor. It was given me by a Swiss professor,' she added inconsequently, as if the nationality and occupation of the donor guaranteed the pedigree of the gift. 'Only he didn't tell me what to do with it. . . . Cook it? Eat it raw? Perhaps we should chop it and chew it like a quid of tobacco. What do you think? Here, have a look. . . .'

She untied the bundle to reveal a revolting-looking fungoid growth, venomous in colour and maculated with warts.

'Shall we try it tonight?'

'Let's not, Iris. Better keep it for a rainy day. I'll put it in the fridge.'

'Oh dear! I can't bear the thought of it freezing in there.'

'It will be all right,' I assured her. 'Mushrooms don't mind the cold. The local ones are even called *gelées* and don't appear until the first frost.'

'But frost is a natural cold, quite different from electrically produced ice. . . . Oh well, have your way. I'll console myself with wine.'

So we broached another bottle. By the end of dinner, which was washed down with further consolation, her mind was made up. 'It's now or never,' she said. 'I'm going to have my mushroom as a nightcap.'

She released it from the frigidaire, whipped a schoolboy penknife out of her pocket, sliced up the fibrous flesh on a wooden board, pounded it with a pestle in a mortar, reduced it to a coarse powder, took a pinch of this between finger and thumb,

Quest for the Eventual Tower

raised it to her nostrils, and inhaled deeply. Xan and I were all agog.

'Do stop staring,' she said. 'You make me feel like a cuckoo clock, as though you're waiting for the bird to pop out.' But nothing happened and even a second pinch produced no effect. 'I'm afraid it's not up to snuff!' she sighed. Then a happy thought occurred to her: 'But it might work in my sleep! I think I'll go to bed now and rub some on my eyelids to induce a midsummer night's dream.'

There was no sign of her at breakfast next morning, no sign of her even two hours later. I was worried but could not bring myself to disturb her. All the same, it was a relief when she eventually appeared looking remarkably spry.

'Any dreams?' I enquired.

'None,' she confessed. 'I slept tight... *very* tight.'

From then on her daily quest for a tower coincided with our own house-hunting. Every morning the three of us would drive off, Xan and I in our car, she in hers. Every evening we would come back and compare notes.

'Any luck?'

'No. What about you?'

'None.'

She never came back empty-handed, however. Sometimes she would arrive with a couple of our baker's dartboard-sized loaves clutched to her breast. 'There's nothing like nursing warm bread,' she would say, dusting the flour from the front of her coat. 'It's almost as comforting as carrying a live goose.' At other times she would turn up with a basket, a three-pronged hay-fork or a wooden tub which she had found in one of the local markets. And invariably she would produce a crop of mushrooms which she had picked at random that day. Occasionally there were even some edible ones among them.

In the evenings she would read us extracts from the long poem* on which she had been working for over a year:

---

* Subsequently entitled *The Marsh Picnic* (Rampant Lions Press, Cambridge, 1966).

The Rainbow Picnic

> It was the withering lady with the sun on her face
> Who told the others she had found the place:
> A house at the end of marshes, by the sea,
> A great farmhouse left empty....

The 'withering lady', she explained, was herself, and the 'marshes by the sea', as we might have guessed, were those near Cadaques. The poem went on to describe a picnic she organized there with four friends, the 'stranger', the 'tall man', the 'young girl' and the 'beautiful woman'. Between them they plan to buy the derelict building and together restore it to life. In their imagination they see themselves already living there:

> They planted gardens for the bees
> Walled against wind by cypress trees,
> Rooms for work, books to read,
> Fruit for jam, bulls to breed.
> Boats, goats, horses, sheep and cows
> Flamed and bellowed around the house,
> Around the table of the feasting peasants,
> Painters, poets, gypsies with guitars,
> While naked swimmers in the phosphorescence
> Splashed through diamonds and stars.

But, as the picnic progresses, they all have second thoughts:

> Each secretly was coveting the place
> Free from the thrall of communal division
> And playfulness had soured into derision
> As they surveyed with speculative gaze
> The barren site, the stricken face of stone
> Counting the cost of every feature gone,
> Undid the fabric of their former praise
> And ran the ruin down.

At which:

> The withering lady felt as on the Ark
> Perplexed that plans should fail
> When Noah's doves were ravens on the gale.

Then a shepherd appears:

Quest for the Eventual Tower

> The black dog barked, the lady waved her hand
> Delighted by his rags, his willow wand,
> The piebald flocks he drove across the dunes
> With goading stones and whistling tunes.

But he too proves a disappointment. Far from being the romantic character he appears, he invites the picknickers to join him in a criminal partnership:

> He babbled on of foreigners he met
> Who stole the chickens and a lamb from fold.
> They too could steal the fattest to be sold,
> Smuggled by car and roasted out of sleep,
> The distant master did not count his sheep
> Nor watch by night; together they could eat
> And share the spoils of money and of meat....

Nothing comes of this, of course; nor does any of the characters ever acquire the house, which eventually falls into the hands of speculators:

> The house is under pavement, and a row
> Of balconied apartments face the beach.
> Far out at sea where bathers cannot reach
> The straggling waters of the marsh are trained
> In channelled sewerage pipes discreetly drained.
> Balloons and motorboats and cars,
> Boutiques and quaintly decorated bars
> Signal for more around the half-moon bay
> Neon to neon wheel to wheel away
> Until all sound of sea, all sight of land
> Are lost as once in whorlings of the sand
> The print of naked feet that led the fray.

Meanwhile her quest for a house seemed no more successful than ours. Xan and I found something which we thought would suit her perfectly: a large cottage flanked by sentinel cypresses and surrounded by a garden of honeysuckle, lavender and rosemary watered by a little stream. But when we took her to see it she shook her head: 'No. . . . Too tame. . . . It might be in Cheshire. . . .'

The Rainbow Picnic

One day, for a change, I let Xan reconnoitre on his own and drove off with her and Aguri in the blue beetle. Not until then did I realize how invaluable this vehicle was to her, for it served not only as a means of locomotion but also as a wardrobe and store-room. Goods and chattels, cardboard boxes, paper bags and books occupied the whole of the back, and Aguri had somehow learnt to confine his large body into an impossibly small space. He was an endearing dog and even strangers appreciated his charm. When we stopped for a drink at a café outside Avignon – unable to resist its name, *Le Tout Va Bien* – the owner promptly presented him with a freshly cooked steak.

In the foothills of the Alpilles we found the sort of house Iris really liked: a huge derelict silkworm farm on the banks of a swift-flowing river, with broad acres and a superb view. To her delight it proved to be for sale and she at once imagined herself installed in it: 'It'll have a tower for a library. The walls will be all books, and there'll be three desks.' But even as she said this she must have known it would never come true, since the price asked was well beyond the means of Diana Cooper or Ivan who wished to provide her with a suitable home 'for the mellow years'.

A few days later, having by now dismissed the silkworm farm from her mind, she came back earlier than usual and announced: 'I've found something at last!'

'Iris! How wonderful!'

'Yes, but wait till you hear what it is! The tower of a mediaeval leper colony!'

'No!' I said, trying to introduce into my tone a note of enthusiasm which I did not feel. For I knew the tower in question, a pencil-thin minaret which I had seen several times from every angle during our excursions. Certainly it was romantic to look at, and possibly also to live in, but only if one was prepared to spend the rest of one's life standing upright, since there was not sufficient room to sit or lie down. Not wishing to be a wet blanket, however, I refrained from pointing out this obvious disadvantage and merely asked, 'Are you sure it's for sale?'

'I haven't the faintest. I only know there's nothing else I

want. . . . But that's not all. Hold on to your hats now! I've found something for *you* as well, something which *is* for sale. It's called the Galerie des Pâtres – there's a fine pastoral-poetic name for you – and it has a loft full of pigeons, and a courtyard with a big tree, and a *bergerie* for the beasts, and an old wine press. . . . But you'd better go and look for yourselves.'

We did go, first thing in the morning, and by the evening had clinched the deal. But we found Iris despondent. The leper tower was not for sale. 'Just as well,' I told her. 'I'm sure you can find something better.'

'No, it's the only thing I wanted,' she replied. 'I shan't go on searching any more in this area. I think I'll try the Pyrenees next.' She brightened at the prospect of further gipsy life. 'There's no point in wasting time. I'll pack tonight and start off early in the morning.'

'I wonder why she's chosen the Pyrenees,' I said to Xan, as we watched her drive away next day.

'Maybe it's good mushroom country,' he suggested.

14 Last Picnic Grounds

Iris never reached the Pyrenees. The next letter I had from her, only a few days after her departure, was posted in Geneva where she had gone to see her doctor. This surprised me, for she had always seemed buoyant with physical well-being. Admittedly, while staying with us, she had often complained of sleeping badly, but had attributed this to indigestion – 'I don't think it's wise to eat cauliflower *au gratin* last thing at night.' Colitis had now been diagnosed, however, and she had been prescribed a macrobiotic diet in conjunction with a course of injections of a serum made from the urine of pregnant mares and the extract of apricot kernels. Worst of all, she had been forbidden cigarettes, coffee and wine. 'I feel a traitor,' she wrote, 'abandoning Bacchus the Mind-Shaker and Ganymede the Cup-Bearer.'

But there was good news as well. She had been lent a studio flat in Cagnes by Kathleen Moffat, Curtis's widow, and was looking forward to spending the winter there, alone with Aguri, to finish her long poem and recover her health. Better still, Friedrich had agreed to drive her there in the blue beetle and they would both be coming to stay with us on the way.

In due course they arrived. It was ten years since I had seen him, and I was delighted to find that his magnificent physique and looks had survived and indeed improved. He was on his way to Rome, to act in another Fellini film. He loved his work,

Last Picnic Grounds

although some of the parts he had played would have been extremely arduous for any other actor of his age. His last role, as a lion-man in a dream sequence, had required him to shin up a ten-metre pole on to a small platform and crouch there while the wind-machine blew a storm of sawdust round him. Iris was obviously very proud of him and, in his company, she too seemed younger than ever.

No sooner had she reached Cagnes, after wishing Friedrich God-speed to Rome, than worry set in. Some weeks previously, her grand-daughter, Lorna Moffat, had set out from Cadaques to ride all the way to the Camargue, but had failed to report her arrival to her father, as arranged. By this time Ivan was understandably anxious and had asked Iris to make enquiries locally. So she promptly got in touch with us. We put out feelers, but to no avail. Then, one morning, our friend Edmond Colomb de Daunant was surprised to find a slender monkish figure standing beside a horse in the courtyard of his house at Nîmes. His eyes were immediately drawn to the small, exquisitely formed, but filthy dirty pair of bare feet protruding from the hem of the coarse homespun habit. Then he noticed a lock of golden hair that had strayed from under the hood, so that he was not entirely surprised when the figure, after fumbling through various pockets, eventually produced a crumpled postcard, a reproduction of a painting by Dali of his wife Gala as the Virgin Mary, on the back of which was written in French: 'Treat Lorna Moffat as such, give her all the help and protection she may need. She is making her legend. Salvador.'

Normally Iris would have felt nothing but sympathy and admiration for someone making such a pilgrimage, but she could not help being rather cross with Lorna for causing Ivan so much worry and wrote to Virginia: 'It would be better if she went to England and started a riding establishment at Longleat* for the trippers.'

Meanwhile she was not enjoying Cagnes as much as she had hoped. The season was over, many of the shops and restaurants were closed, the mistral whistled through the narrow streets and the little town had a sad, deserted, almost sinister air. She

* The marquess of Bath's house in Wiltshire, open to the public.

imagined hostile eyes peering at her through the shuttered windows of the empty houses, and hated the sight of the little bags of rat poison hanging from lintels and drainpipes. To make matters worse, Aguri enraged the neighbours by harrying their cats, and Iris feared some sort of retaliation. She woke up one morning to find that the blue beetle, parked in a side street, had been stolen with all it contained: several books, typescripts of plays, unfinished articles, her precious mushroom chart, bits and pieces of clothing that she hadn't yet unloaded and, worst of all, the first part of the long poem on which she was still at work. She herself found several pages of her manuscript lying in a ditch, and others fluttering in the branches of a nearby tree. The police eventually recovered the car; but the car papers, left in the glove-box, had vanished.

On learning of this disaster, a friend of Kathleen Moffat's, the author Diana Holman-Hunt, who had just arrived from England to stay in her own holiday house on the edge of the village, called at once to see if she could be of any help. She had not yet met Iris, so was not prepared for the shock she received from the apparition standing at the top of the stairs in a long dark robe, with hair that in the half light had assumed the colour of ashes, and face deathly white.

'I can't swallow,' Iris croaked, holding her throat. She was clearly very ill.

I heard about her plight that evening when an American friend of ours, Kenneth Pender, rang up to say that he was about to drive her to Switzerland, where she could be with Boon and see her own doctor. Since she wanted me to look after Aguri for her and also harbour the beetle, he planned to deliver both as soon as he could. A few days later Iris's black familiar was happily installed in the house he already knew: and the little car, still crammed with what was left of her worldly possessions, safely stowed away in the wood-shed.

Meanwhile her doctor decided she must have an immediate operation, and Boon advised her to go back to London for it. She knew this was bound to be painful, but what she dreaded most was 'the marring of the marble' of her body. Diana Cooper engaged a tip-top surgeon and got her into the King Edward VII

9a) Ivan Moffat at Castle MacGarrett

9b) Iris and Oonagh Oranmore

9c) Iris, Boon and Captain Eric Meiville

10a) Iris in Rome

10b) Iris reading 'Tiger, tiger, burning bright

11) Iris and Aguri, her Belgian sheepdog, at Montalivet, the 'last picnic ground'

12) Last photograph of Iris by Cecil Beaton

Last Picnic Grounds

Hospital, normally reserved for officers and their dependents, where a large part of her colon was removed. For several days her condition was critical, but her urchin grin was never entirely extinguished, despite the horror of tubes up her nostrils, saline drips and blood transfusions – 'bourgeois blood,' she objected. 'I would have preferred horse or tiger to fiercen me.'

In California Ford Rainey, Daphne Field and many other friends waited anxiously for the outcome. Telegrams of good wishes and sympathy poured in from all over the world. So many flowers were sent that her room could not hold them all. In Cadaques, at Meliton's, the news that she was out of danger was celebrated by a round of free drinks.

For some time before being released from hospital, she had to undergo a course of cobalt ray treatment which left her exhausted. She was also depressed to hear that she was expected to lead the life of an invalid for the next year. Nevertheless she at once started planning ahead. She arranged for Aguri to be collected by her friend Gitte Rey and taken back to Cadaques, and asked me if I could somehow get the blue beetle to Geneva where she hoped to pick it up in due course. By this time the little car was a real 'hot potato', unlicensed, uninsured and in a bad state of repair, but I managed to persuade an intrepid young acquaintance to carry out the mission. Meanwhile Iris went to convalesce at Job's Mill, where she was cossetted by Virginia, then came back to stay with Diana Cooper in London.

One evening, as she and Diana were about to leave for the opera, the front-door bell rang. She went to see who was there, whereupon three men, with nylon stockings pulled over their faces, burst into the the house. Thinking this was a practical joke, she laughed: 'Very good disguises. Who are you? See if I can guess.' She began reeling off the names of various friends, but was roughly silenced. She realized the intruders meant business when the man-servant, on coming up from the basement, was promptly knocked unconscious. She was then bundled upstairs into Diana's room, where both of them were ordered to lie on the bed, while their legs were shackled and their hands tied behind their backs with Diana's own belts hanging conveniently in the cupboard.

The Rainbow Picnic

Both of them kept their heads and showed no fear. Iris even tried to reason with the men, asking what had driven them to crime. They told her to shut up and turn her face to the wall. Two of them then ransacked the house, while the third stayed behind on guard. At one moment he picked up Iris's handbag and shook out its contents. 'Who steals my purse steals trash,' she quoted, as a handful of coppers, a lipstick, a pencil-stub and a sixpenny notebook spilled on to the floor.

The burglars found no valuables and at last made off, their total swag amounting to some very petty cash, a fur coat of Diana's and her car which had been parked outside the house. The two victims were left, in Diana's own words, 'trussed up like fowls for roasting', but she eventually managed to free her hands, hop to the telephone with her ankles still bound, and apologize to the friends who had been kept waiting. 'Sorry, but we got rather tied up,' she said.

Though Iris showed such remarkable composure during the ordeal, she was still rather shaky after her operation and consequently suffered from delayed nervous shock. Haunted by the memory of those featureless faces under the nylon masks, she was unable to sleep and longed to be out of London, which she now found sinister. She therefore crossed over to Ireland and spent Easter with her friend John Huston, the film director: '. . . exceedingly comfortable and easy, surrounded by great Mexican gods and trays of Jameson's whisky, with the green outside more like a back-drop than a brisk walk,' as she wrote to Maud Russell. 'Riding days are well nigh over, alack!'

From here she went to stay with Oonagh Oranmore who, since the break-up of her marriage, had left Castle MacGarrett and was now living at Luggala, a Victorian Gothic folly, bequeathed to her by her father Ernest Guinness. Iris revelled in the beauty of the surroundings: the great lake of peat-brown water, the oatmeal-coloured strand glistening with mica, mountains mauve with young heather. Since the house was overflowing with young people assembled for the twenty-first birthday party of Oonagh's youngest son, Tara, she was installed in the annexe, built in the style of a Canadian log cabin, where she had a suite to herself. Though it was only a few steps from the main building, she felt nervous going across there in the dark and Oonagh saw her back every night to make sure there was no man lurking under the bed, both of them laughing that she, of all people, should succumb to such old-maidish fears.

Her next visit was to her old love Eric Meiville, the Swiss captain, now happily married, whom she had not seen for many years, 'at their nice house near the marvellous stud stables built of tumbled grey abbey stones', as she described it to Maud Russell.

> Sleek yearlings, and foalfull mares knee-deep in straw, and a harness room with a great fireplace and hot whisky and paintings of horses. It was altogether a fireside visit owing to the elements. . . . The captain has grown a little deaf owing to shooting so much in his many wars. It is sad because he is still very quick in reaction though slow of hearing. We finally persuaded him to go to the ear doctor. Both he and his wife are enormously hospitable, generous and romantic.

By the time she returned to England she had recovered her nerve and was able to enjoy 'a party at Murray's firm for Paddy Leigh Fermor's book-christening.* I always love him. Krishnamurti is giving talks in London, which I attend, and May Day with the Bath lions† I look forward to. Further plans I cannot shape because they are rather without goal, that's why reading is so nice, and the people in the books do the shaping and goaling with breathless activity, while we follow them hazily from the pillow.'

Her companion on the May Day visit was Patrick Crosse, whose wife, Jenny Nicholson, had died a couple of years before, her death being commemorated by Iris in a poem ending with the lovely lines:

> Midsummer fold you in its arms this wintry day
> You were a dancer
> Sleep as you rise
> Spinning and lost in light.

---

* Patrick Leigh Fermor, *Roumeli* (John Murray, 1966).
† The pride of lions, kept in natural surroundings at Longleat.

The Rainbow Picnic

In her bread-and-butter letter to Virginia, she wrote:

> We had a smooth and easy journey back and watched parachutes fall like convolvuli, but I'm rather angry with England for providing no tea-rooms now. We stopped at a promising inn on the river near Staines, and the desk-girl said, 'Oh no, we don't serve tea. Why, we'd be packed! I don't know where you'd get *tea* . . . not on Sundays!' 'When else?' I said and left with the feeling that Mrs Wilfred's tea-gardens no longer lived nor her home-made jams; that muffins were dead, crumpets forgotten and scones all buried with Mrs Wilfred under the asphalt orchards. There was, however, a café painted in demon-red and black with horrid shelves to drink at from paper cups and cellophane sandwiches of cardboard ham.

'I long for somewhere wild,' she wrote again a little later, 'another planet – patience!' Atlantic rather than Mediterranean shores now attracted her and in June she left for Paris, where she was met by Friedrich who had meanwhile collected Aguri from Cadaques and the blue beetle from Geneva. Together they drove south,

> through Poitiers, stopping at a charming river-glade place called La Garette in the *marée* with canals and pleasure-boats plying between trees among reeds and ducks. It claims to be 'La Venise Verte'; there are inns on the bank for eel-eating. The food is astoundingly good.
>
> There are oysters and all fish in plenty, a completely deserted endless stretch of yellow beach, dunes backed by pine forests wherein grow flowing clumps of mead, and there are clearings of little farms.
>
> I love it here in the Gironde, heart of Medoc and the wines of Bordeaux.

At Montalivet Friedrich found her a small villa, where he stayed with her a few days before returning to Austria. But she was not left entirely alone. Boon was staying in a nudist camp on the coast a few miles away, with his 'beautiful but Beatle-minded son Marius'. She was not pleased, however, with the glimpse she had of the 'dreary camp of naked Germans with no high life, only pot, pop, pep, pornography, promiscuity, and all that adolescence requires of life today. . . . The Chelsea Pensioners are gayer, in scarlet and medals, with their pints of bitter. . . . My own plans are not quite decided, either Gstaad in a week for a month or so, or stay here and really explore the Gironde, the Landes, the sea.'

Friends visited her from time to time; and Virginia had arranged for her daughter Georgia Tennant to dart out at a moment's notice and take her to Spain should she wish to see Gitte Rey and her cronies at Cadaques. All this was a great comfort to her. 'And one blue day Friedrich will come,' she wrote in her letter of thanks. Meanwhile she spent several hours every day at a local café, the Bijou Bar, where she read and dealt with her correspondence since she even used it as a postal address. Cafés had always been a source of enjoyment to her, and the absence of them in England was one of the reasons why she preferred to live abroad.

One morning her mail contained a delightful surprise: a copy of her long poem *The Marsh Picnic*, beautifully printed on woven paper and bound in sand-coloured hard covers, with the title in handsome saffron lettering on a pale yellow label. Unbeknown to her, an edition of three hundred had been produced at the instigation of Diana and a number of other friends. Nothing could have given her greater pleasure, and her sense of achievement increased when she read John Betjeman's introduction:

This strangely haunting poem . . . belongs to the age of the 1920s and early 30s, both in phraseology and outlook. This is because it is the sincere expression by its creator who is a fastidious and experienced poet. It is therefore a joy to greet it, instead of in the typescript and photostat copies which have been handed round by its admirers, in the distinguished typography of the Rampant Lions Press.

A spate of congratulatory letters followed, including one from David Cecil:

The Rainbow Picnic

> I think your poem is perfectly lovely. It has a double beauty. It is a lovely thing in itself, an intricate, melodious pattern of word and image: you make me see the old house and the sea and the sullen weather. I love the end too, although it is sad – the contrast between what the place was at the time of the poem and what it has been turned into now. Everything passes, everything fades; yet your poem makes one accept this because you turn it into something beautiful.

Encouraged, she embarked on a series of word portraits of famous people she had known and loved, such as her father and Augustus John. She completed these articles in record time, writing very fast as though she feared the sands might run out before she had finished her task. But only one of them was published. The rest disappeared without trace in circumstances she described when appealing a few weeks later to the editor of *The Southampton Echo*:

> Dear Sir,
>
> I should be extremely grateful if any of your readers could give some clue in my search for a young man from Southampton neighbourhood who worked this summer in Bordeaux, France. He is tall, slender, wears glasses and is interested in painting as a hobby.
>
> I am a writer and had completed two long stories at Montalivet – a seaside resort – where I met him towards the end of August. He very kindly volunteered to type certain corrections and several poems, to be returned to me on his next visit. I was so hurriedly grateful that I gave him the whole lot, my only copies, but neglected to ask for his name and address.
>
> He probably came back while I was briefly visiting friends elsewhere and failed to trace my whereabouts. After a month of waiting in vain I failed to trace him in Bordeaux – a large city bestrewn with Englishmen apprenticed to the wine trade, etc.
>
> Whoever has heart- and head-ached their way through prose or verse will understand how deeply the loss of these finally completed scripts is felt, especially when they are awaited by a publisher.

Last Picnic Grounds

My last piece, a memoir, appeared in the 'London Magazine' and the young man read it on the occasion we met.

This letter is a shot in the dark, but perhaps it may reach some light or response from the 'Southampton Echo'.

Urgently, hopefully and respectfully yours,

Iris Tree.

By this time she had lost a great deal of weight, but was still strong enough to take Aguri for walks in the pine woods, where she enjoyed talking to a forester who lived in a hut and had a reputation among the local peasants as a healer. Another source of great pleasure to her was the discovery of a small vineyard dotted with pear trees, on which she cast a covetous eye. Many of her friends, however, were worried about her, notably Diana who wrote:

> I think about you most of the time, what with prayers and hopes and fears, so send me occasionally a postcard truthfully written.

Virginia, too, felt concern and sent her presents from time to time, which she acknowledged with childlike delight:

> How charming it was to receive the little face-brush wrapped up in honey and a ten-pound note. Nursery rhymes do come true!

Sometimes, in answer to anxious inquiries, she even described her health as 'good'. But she admitted to a dwindling physical force, a feeling that autumn had come upon her after a long summer.

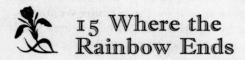# 15 Where the Rainbow Ends

Iris was born in London and, as she felt the tide of her life ebbing, she returned there to complete the circle, staying with Ivan and his wife Kate* in their garden-house in Tregunter Road and sleeping in Ivan's dressing-room.

Her Pied Piper charm had already won the heart of her four-year-old grandson, Jonathan, who called her 'Nona' and would come to see her as soon as she was awake and to say goodnight before he went to bed, asking her to tell him one more story.

She conserved her strength by resting as much as possible, reading in bed, contemplating and writing letters. She also started a last poem:

> Bury me under a tree
> Because of my name and ancestry
> Because all trees are suppliants of light
> Give shade by day and flame of fires by night...

Her room was always filled with flowers including her favourite yellow and white roses, which Raimund von Hofmannsthal sent daily. Over her bed she had pinned a gift from Nigel Ryan – a Mexican sunflower head made of paper, which presided over her room like a miniature sun.

* Formerly the Hon. Kathleen Smith.

Where the Rainbow Ends

Ivan spent much time with her, telling her the latest gossip from the film world, describing how he and Kate had spent the previous evening, using his talent of mimicry to bring before her the people they had met, his wit and play on words reminding her of her father and Uncle Max.

Sometimes she went out to lunch at a restaurant with a close friend – Patrick Crosse, Raimund or Nigel – treats to which she eagerly looked forward and for which she took great trouble over her appearance. Occasionally she also went to the theatre, but this proved too arduous for her; during one performance she fainted and had to be carried out to an ambulance.

When her sister Felicity came to see her, they relived their days at Brancaster (where Felicity now lived), laughing at their rivalry over Evelyn Beerbohm, trying to remember the words of the cockney songs he had taught them on the nursery piano at 77 Sloane Street.

In October 1967 I was in London recuperating from an operation on my leg, lying-up on a sofa in my daughter's house, where Iris was brought by Judy Gendell to spend the afternoon with me.

I had not seen her for three years. She was very thin and wore a full bright blue coat, boldly checkered in orange, which she kept wrapped round her all the time. Over her shoulder was slung the poacher's bag we had bought together in Languedoc. Her immaculate brown shoes were buckled in gold. Under the broad brim of a russet-coloured felt hat, her face looked luminous.

I can't remember what we talked about since I had been given pain-killing drugs which fogged my memory for a while. But I still feel in retrospect the calm glow of her presence. This was the last time I saw her.

Costa Achillopoulos, who saw her six months later, was equally struck by her looks and, although he knew how ill she had been, thought she had miraculously recovered and suggested taking her for a drive in the country some time during the following week.

'But I shall be dead by then,' she replied. Meanwhile she worried about the vineyard in the Gironde. 'Can't see how to get back to those pear trees and plant others.'

The Rainbow Picnic

In due course Friedrich and Boon came to England to be with her, and their tall figures towered by her bedside like Gog and Magog. At night Friedrich slept on the floor in her room. She continued to write letters and, although her strength was ebbing, her handwriting was as firm as ever, and her wit as lovely. To Gitte Rey she confided: *'Comme Pierrot ma chandelle est presque morte.'* She also continued to have visitors but now, after talking for a while, she would dismiss them gently, not because she was tired but in order to indulge in contemplation. 'You must go now,' she told a friend who had come to see her the day before she died, 'I don't want to break the web of my thoughts.'

That evening, when her nurse, about to give her an injection, said brightly, 'Now then, just a little prick, dear.' Iris looked at her intently, then, switching on her urchin grin, asked: 'Are you sure you're not a hypoprick?'

On 28 April 1968, she drifted into a coma. Friedrich was close beside her. She regained consciousness briefly and recognized him. Stretching out her arms, as though seeing a vision, she spoke her last words:

'It's here, it's here. . . . Shining. . . . Love. . . . Love. . . . Love.'

Index

Index

Index

Achillopoulos, Costa, 129, 153
Aguri, Iris's Belgian sheepdog, 122, 126, 132, 135, 142, 144, 145, 148, 151
Alexander, Jacqueline, 35
Allen, Kathleen, see Moffat, Kathleen
Alma-Tadema, Sir Lawrence, 31
Ansell, Gracie, 107
Anson, Dennis, 56
Aragon, Louis, 82
Asquith, Herbert, 28, 38, 39, 56
Asquith, Mrs Herbert (née Margot Tennant), 27, 28, 38, 46
Asquith, Raymond, 45, 54

Bankhead, Tallulah, 80
Bath, marchioness of (née Virginia Parsons), 11, 71, 81, 101, 104n, 124, 128, 143, 145, 148, 149, 151
Bath, marquess of, 99n, 124, 143n
Beerbohm, Agnes, 21, 23
Beerbohm, Constance, 24
Beerbohm, Dora, 21, 23, 106, 116
Beerbohm, Evelyn, 55, 56
Beerbohm, Herbert; see Tree, Sir Herbert
Beerbohm, Julius (Herbert's brother), 23
Beerbohm, Julius (Herbert's father), 19, 20, 21
Beerbohm, Mrs Julius, I (née Constantia Draper), 21; II (née Eliza Draper), 21
Beerbohm, Sir Max, 21, 23, 29n, 40, 73, 116, 122
Bell, Clive, 12, 57–9
Bell, Dr Quentin, 12
Bell, Vanessa, 52
Benckendorff, Constantine, 56
Benson, F. R., 25
Betjeman, Sir John, 12, 149
Betjeman, Lady (née Penelope Chetwode), 197
Bischofsheim, Mrs, 30

Carrington, Dora, 48–9, 52, 57, 121
Cassel, Sir Ernest, 30
Cecil, Sir David, 12, 21n, 122n, 149
Chaplin, Charles, 61–2, 117
Chekhov, Michael, 111, 112, 115
Chetwode, Penelope; see Betjeman, Lady
Cleveland, President, 28
Cole, Horace de Vere, 55
Collier, Constance, 60, 61, 71
Colomb de Daunant, Edmond, 143
Cooper, Lady Diana, 11, 32 and n, 33, 37, 44, 56n, 86–91, 94, 95, 120, 126, 131–3, 140, 144, 145, 146, 149, 151
Cooper, Duff, 53, 86, 89, 101, 120

Index

Cory-Wright, Sir Geoffrey, 67
Cory-Wright, Lady (*née* Felicity
  Tree), 11, 29, 33, 34, 37, 40, 55,
  153
Crosse, Patrick, 122, 129, 147, 153
Cunard, Nancy, 35, 49, 80, 81, 82–3,
  125, 135

Dali, Salvador, 133, 143
Daly, Bose, 108
Daly, Diana, 108–9
Draper, Constantia; *see* Beerbohm,
  Mrs Julius (I)
Draper, Eliza; *see* Beerbohm, Mrs
  Julius (II)
Du Maurier, Gerald 79–80, 101

Elsie, Lily, 28
Epstein, Jacob, 52
Eyres-Monsell, Joan; *see* Leigh
  Fermor, The Hon. Mrs

Fedorovitch, Sophie, 83
Field, Daphne, 11, 113, 115, 117,
  118, 145
Fielding, Xan, 12, 125, 133, 137,
  139–41
Fortescue, Lady, *There's Rosemary
  ... There's Rue*, 32n
France, Anatole, 28
Fripp, Sir Alfred, 72
Fry, Roger, 52

Garbo, Greta, 102, 117
Garnett, David, 81n
Gendell, Milton, 123
Gendell, Mrs Milton (*née* Judy
  Montagu), 123, 153
Gilbert, W. S., 25, 26
Gish, Lillian, 102, 117
Glyn, Elinor, 91
Granby, Lady; *see* Rutland,
  duchess of
Grant, Duncan, 52
Graves, Robert, 122, 129
Grenfell, Julian and Billy, 56, 104n
Guevara, Alvaro, 52

Harkness, Alan, 114, 115, 116, 117,
  118
Hart-Davis, Deirdre, 75, 76

Hart-Davis, Richard, 54, 75–6
Hart-Davis, Mrs Richard (*née* Sybil
  Cooper), 53–5, 62, 65, 75, 80, 84,
  86
Hart-Davis, Sir Rupert, 11, 75–6
Henley, W. C., 32
Hill, Derek, 123
Hofmannsthal, Alice (*née* Astor), 99
Hofmannsthal, Raimund von, 88,
  99, 104, 152, 153
Holman-Hunt, Diana, 144
Holt, Maud; *see* Tree, Lady
Horner, Edward, 56, 104n
Huston, John, 146
Hutchinson, St John, 107
Huxley, Aldous, 128, 131

John, Augustus, 52, 55, 57, 60, 83–4
John, Dorelia, 83–4
John, Poppet, 84
John, Romilly, 84
John, Vivian, 84

Kelly, David, 123
Keynes, Maynard, 57
Kommer, Dr Rudolf (Kaetchen),
  87–9, 92–4, 95
Krishnamurti, 116, 128, 147

Ledebur, Dr Christian (Boon), 11,
  94, 95, 96, 102, 115, 116, 128, 144,
  154
Ledebur, Count Friedrich, 11, 91,
  92–6, 99–102, 104, 106, 108–9, 111,
  113–14, 117, 121, 124–5, 148, 154
Leigh, Fermor, The Hon. Mrs (*née*
  Joan Eyres-Monsell), 107
Leverson, Ada, 79
Lewis, Sir George, 27
Lewis, Mrs Rosa, 50
Lister, Charles, 56
Lygon, Lady Dorothy, 129

Macnamara, Francis, 84
Manners, Diana; *see* Cooper, Lady
  Diana
Manners, Marjorie, 38
Marsh, Edward, 64
Meiville, Eric, 108, 118, 147
Mendelssohn, Elenore, 99

Index

Menuhin, Yehudi, 128
Meyer, Carl, 30
Moffat, Curtis, 66, 69, 75, 77, 81, 82, 92, 94, 95, 103, 121, 129
Moffat, Ivan, 11, 71, 81, 83, 89, 90, 91, 95, 96, 102, 103, 117, 140, 152, 153
Moffat, Mrs Ivan (née The Hon. Kathleen Smith), 152, 153
Moffat, Kathleen (née Allen), 103–4, 129, 142, 144
Moffat, Lorna, 143
Montagu, Judy; see Gendell, Mrs Milton
Moore, George, 80
Morell, Lady Ottoline, 52
Morphet, Richard, 12, 129–31
Munby, Dr A. N. L., 12

Neilson, Julia, 26
Nelkie, Maud; see Russell, Mrs Gilbert
Nicholson, Jenny (Mrs Patrick Crosse), 122, 129, 142
Nicholson, William, 47

Oranmore and Browne, Oonagh Lady, 12, 108, 146–7

Palfy, Count, 120n
Parsons, Alan, 40, 78–9, 80, 102
Parsons, Mrs Alan (née Viola Tree), 13, 25, 26, 33, 34, 37, 38, 40–3, 64–5, 71, 78–9, 80, 101, 102, 104, 105, 112–13
Parsons, David, 123
Parsons, Virginia; see Bath, marchioness of
Pearson, Hesketh, 12
Pender, Kenneth, 144

Rainey, Ford, 117, 118, 145
Reinhardt, Max, 86, 87
Rey, Gitte, 145, 149, 154
Ribblesdale, Lord, 38, 39, 50, 56, 57
Robertson, Graham, 37
Rothschild, Lord, 30
Russell, Bertrand, 57
Russell, Mrs Gilbert (née Maud Nelkie), 11, 36, 41, 47, 48, 82, 102, 106, 114, 122, 147

Rutland, duchess of, 27, 33, 36, 107

Sayers, Mrs Eileen, 11
Schwelter, Maria, 40, 41, 43
Shaw, Bernard, 31
Shaw-Stewart, Patrick, 56, 104n
Simon, André, 103
Sitwell, Osbert, 103
Smail, Penelope, 129
Smith, The Hon. Kathleen; see Moffat, Mrs Ivan
Solano, Solita, 12, 63–4, 73
Stevenson, Robert Louis, 32
Strachey, Lytton, 81n
Streaight, Beatrice, 113, 117
Symons, A. J., 82, 103

Tennant, Margot; see Asquith, Mrs Herbert
Terry, Ellen, 37
Tree, Felicity; see Cory-Wright, Lady
Tree, Sir Herbert, 19, 20, 21, 22, 23, 24, 25, 26, 27–8, 30–2, 38, 45–6, 60–1, 62–7, 71–2, 73
Tree, Lady (née Maud Holt), 19, 20, 21, 22, 23, 24–6, 27–8, 31, 32, 33, 37, 39, 43, 45, 46–7, 48, 75, 77, 81–2, 95, 112
Tree, Iris, birth, 29; family influence on, 13; meets author, 13; childhood, 32–4, 37, 40; school, 34–6; early poem, 39; in Milan, 41–3; art student, 44, 48–9; banished to the country, 47; love of animals, 50; self-portrait in verse, 50–2; sits for portraits, 52; *In Praise of Augustus John*, 53n; with Horace de Vere Cole, 55; with 'Corrupt Coterie', 56; link with Bloomsbury, 57–8; with father in America, 60–3; poem read at Georgian Poetry Society, 64–5; meets Curtis Moffat, 66; marries him, 67; honeymoon, 69; poem to Curtis, 70–1; birth of Ivan, 71; poem to father, 73–4; back in England, 75–7; friendship with Nancy Cunard, 80–1; in Paris, 82–3; in Dorset, 83–4; auditioned for *The Miracle*,

Index

86–7; on tour in America, 87–90; meets Friedrich Ledebur, 91; life with him, 92–3; *The Traveller*, 93; birth of Boon, 94; divorces Curtis, 95; meets author, 99; at Kammer, 100; at Rottingdean, 101; back to California, 102; return to England, 104–5; in Ireland, 106–8; hunting in France, 109; Chekhov Theatre Studio, 111; mother's death, 112; Viola's death, 113; with Chekhov Studio in America, 114–16; *Sing About It*, 115; *Second Wind*, 117; poem for Eric Meiville, 118–19; return to Europe, 120; death of Curtis, 121; divorces Friedrich, 121; in Rome, 121–3; *Strangers' Wharf*, 123–4; in *Dolce Vita*, 125; in Venice, 125–6; in Greece, 126–7; nomadic life, 128–9; in London, 129–31; in Portugal, 131–3; in Cadaques, 133–4; house-hunting in Languedoc, 135–41; *The Marsh Picnic*, 137–9, 149–51, in Cagnes, 142–4; operation in London, 144–5; attacked by burglars, 145–6; in Ireland, 146–7; poem to Jenny Nicholson, 147; at Montalivet, 148–51; article in *London Magazine*, 151; back to London, 152–3; death, 154

Tree, Viola; *see* Parsons, Mrs Alan

Vilmorin, Louise de, 120–1

Walker, Romaine, 31
Waller, Lewis, 45
Weymouth, Viscount (now marquess of Bath), 99n
Wilde, Oscar, 32, 79
Wilson, Sir Matthew (Scatters), 56–7
Wolff, Miss, 35, 36
Wyndham, Olivia, 82
Wyndham, Richard, 82
Wyndham, Viola, *The Sphinx and Her Circle*, 79n